The essence of Herefordshire: the cattle have taken the county name around the globe, the apples supply the world's largest cider works.

Shire County Guide 16
HEREFORDSHIRE
and the Black Mountains

Barry R. Freeman

Shire Publications Ltd

CONTENTS

1. The frontier land 3
2. The countryside 6
3. Places of archaeological interest 11
4. Castles and monastic ruins 13
5. Churches and chapels 17
6. Historic houses and gardens 23
7. Museums and other places of interest 29
8. Cider 34
9. A county calendar 37
10. Herefordshire people 39
11. Towns and villages 42
12. Tourist information centres 54
Map of Herefordshire and the Black
Mountains 55
Index 56

Set in 8 point Times roman and printed in Great Britain by C. I. Thomas and Sons (Haverfordwest) Ltd, Press Buildings, Merlins Bridge, Haverfordwest, Dyfed.

British Library Cataloguing in Publication Data available.

ACKNOWLEDGEMENTS

The publishers wish to acknowledge the assistance of Miss A. E. Sandford BA AMA, Curator of Hereford City Museum and Art Gallery. The county map and Hereford street plan are by D. R. Darton. Photographs are acknowledged as follows: Sharon Boulton, pages 10, 11, 19, 20, 22 (upper), 25, 26, 27, 38 and 54; H. P. Bulmer plc, pages 1, 30, 34, 35 and 36; Kathleen Freeman, cover and pages 3, 4, 9, 13, 15, 16, 21, 22 (lower), 23, 24, 41, 42, 43, 44, 45, 51 and 52; Hereford Herd Book Society, page 37; Cadbury Lamb, pages 7, 14, 17, 29, 32, 33, 46, 49, 50 and 53.

NOTE

Since 1974 Herefordshire has been combined with Worcestershire to form the administrative County of Hereford and Worcester. This book covers the old county and also some adjacent areas of Gwent and Powys, in Wales, in order that the whole of the Black Mountains may be included.

MAP REFERENCES

Map references in this book are for the Ordnance Survey 1:50,000 Landranger series. They are given as a sheet number followed by the six-figure reference. The prefix SO is omitted, being common to all references quoted. Where map sheets overlap, a frequent occurrence in this area, more than one sheet number is provided.

COVER: *The river Arrow at Eardisland.*

The beautiful Vale of Ewyas is the eastern gateway to the Black Mountains.

1
The frontier land

It is not easy for the modern visitor to realise the original importance of the Marcher, or border, counties, as we have been accustomed to the peaceful union of England and Wales since the time of Henry VIII. But for almost fifteen hundred years Herefordshire was a frontier region, often an expendable buffer zone between prosperous lowland England and rugged untamed Wales. Romans, Saxons and Normans all found their conquering advances brought to a halt against the eastern slopes of the Welsh uplands and preferred to consolidate their territorial gains before pushing heavily armed exploratory columns further westward.

Once the Acts of Union had taken effect, by the middle of the sixteenth century, Herefordshire settled peacefully into its agricultural role, broken only briefly by the Civil War. Remote from the coalfields and main lines of communication, it was virtually unscathed by the industrial revolution and is today one of England's most unspoilt and genuinely rural counties.

Herefordshire began to emerge as an identifiable region during the seventh century, as a western province of the kingdom of Mercia. Successive vigorous rulers, chiefly Penda and Wulfhere, pushed the frontiers of Mercia as far west as the Welsh foothills, at the expense of the neighbouring Kingdom of Powys. Offa, the greatest of the Mercian kings, who ruled from AD 757 to 796, controlled all England south of the Humber and is frequently regarded as the first true king of England. It was a kingdom with far-flung frontiers and a variety of peoples, many of whom were kept in a state of subjection. There were no more unwilling subjects than those in the Welsh borderlands, where the neighbouring dispossessed refugees in Powys were ever ready to carry out armed raids or foster discontent. In this period the massive earthwork of Offa's Dyke was excavated and Hereford emerged as a city of strategic and ecclesiastical importance. Debate exists over the origin of the city name: the generally accepted derivation is that it was a fording point (Welsh *fford,* road) adequate to take an armed company (Saxon *herepath,* a road adequate for an army).

Hereford's strategic importance was the greater because at that time it lay on a

3

The stark outlines of the Black Mountains.

boundary line. South of the Wye were two semi-independent regions, Archenfield and Ewyas, covering most of what is now south Herefordshire and stretching deep into the Black Mountains. The inhabitants were doughty warriors, prized and respected by the Mercian kings as front-line troops against the Welsh.

With Offa's death at the end of the eighth century the power structure in Mercia gradually disintegrated and two centuries of almost unbroken strife, intrigue, alliances and counter-alliances followed, as England was torn apart by civil war and Scandinavian invaders. In the 980s the Danes advanced through Herefordshire, plundering the town and monastery of Leominster, putting the monks to flight and slaying as many of the townspeople as they could find. This mayhem was eventually brought to an end with the Norman conquest, as William the Conqueror tightened his grip on Herefordshire as on the rest of England.

After the Norman conquest, the period of the Lords Marcher began with the most trusted of William's barons being granted vast tracts of land to hold in their sovereign's name on condition they kept his Welsh frontier secure. As they had menaced the Romans and Saxons for a thousand years, so the Welsh presented a continual threat to the new Norman rulers. The Earldom of Hereford was granted to William Fitzosborn, one of King William's closest associates and most trusted

allies. He died in 1072, but in those six years after the Conquest he founded boroughs and built castles at Wigmore, Clifford and numerous other strategic border points as far south as Chepstow.

Yet more centuries of strife ensued, with the Marcher Lords frequently becoming ambitious to extend their power, abandoning the struggle against the Welsh and fighting each other, or even, on several occasions, threatening the monarch. The powerful Mortimer family held the neighbouring strongholds of Wigmore and Ludlow, amongst others, and on the bloody battlefield of Mortimer's Cross in 1461, nineteen-year-old Edward Mortimer, Earl of March, won the day for the Yorkist cause, marched to London and was crowned King Edward IV.

After the Wars of the Roses and the accession of the Tudors peace came to Herefordshire. The Acts of Union in 1534 and 1536 ended the county's role as a frontier region and a long period of agricultural prosperity began, chiefly characterised by the breed of cattle which have carried Hereford's name around the world.

Herefords are an extremely adaptable breed of cattle, able to survive and thrive in the arctic snows of Finland, the heat of the northern Transvaal, the rough pampas of Uruguay or the subtropical regions of Brazil. The origins of the Hereford are believed to lie in a cross between the small red cattle of Roman Britain and the large white Welsh breed once widely distributed along the border lands. The result was a sturdy draught ox; Herefords, like all other breeds, were for many centuries both working animals and beef producers. At the first Smithfield show in 1799, a Hereford ox measured 8 feet 11 inches (2.75 metres) in length, was 6 feet 7 inches (2 metres) high and had a girth of 10 feet 4 inches (3.15 metres): he was sold for 100 guineas (£105). In 1980 a British Hereford bull was sold for 27,000 guineas (£28,350) to a Canadian breeder.

The Hereford Herd Book Society was founded under the patronage of Queen Victoria in 1878 to administer the affairs of the breed and register the pedigree of every purebred Hereford in the British Isles. The herd-book was opened in 1846 and since 1884 has been closed to any animal of which the sire or dam has not been previously entered, to ensure the purity of the breed. Although other new crossbred strains have been introduced in recent years, the sight of a pedigree Hereford herd grazing peacefully in orchard or meadow remains the essential hallmark of the Herefordshire countryside.

Two of Hereford's largest industries are based on agriculture: cidermaking and poultry production.

Herefordshire is almost saucer-shaped — a central lowland area ringed by hills. Hereford itself occupies a strategic position in the centre of the lowlands, where the valleys of the Wye and Lugg converge. All around lie rich farmlands, based on the well drained, glacially deposited soils which form a deep fertile mantle over the Old Red Sandstone rocks.

East of Hereford, along the road leading to Ledbury, is hop country, the tall shelter hedges of the hopyards lining the road on either side. Hops are an important crop in this area, which is second only to Kent in output. Until the 1960s a large migrant labour force, mainly gypsies, would arrive for the hop picking, followed by cider-apple gathering. Most of this work has now disappeared as vine stripping and apple picking have been mechanised.

Around the borders of Herefordshire both rocks and landscape change, and so does the agriculture. Eastwards, beyond Ledbury, the long narrow ridge of the Malvern Hills rises majestically in a chain of undulating summits, providing England's most dramatic line of hills. Because of their exposed aspect, thin soil and steep slopes, sheep grazing is the only practical form of agriculture and the closely cropped turf makes the Malverns superb walking country.

Southwards, past Ross-on-Wye, another change of rock to carboniferous limestone results in the famous gorge at Symonds Yat as the Wye cuts its way down to the Severn estuary and Bristol Channel. Here lowland Herefordshire ends against the northern edge of the Forest of Dean plateau, another area rich in landscape and history.

The Black Mountains form the south-west corner of Herefordshire and extend well into the neighbouring Welsh counties of Gwent and Powys. In a series of parallel valleys there is wonderful country for exploration, crossed by the rivers Dore, Escley, Monnow, Olchon and Honddu, the last named flowing down the beautiful Vale of Ewyas. From the head of the Vale, above the beautiful ruins of Llanthony Abbey, a narrow mountain road climbs to Gospel Pass and the very heart of the Black Mountains, which, like the Malverns, can support only sheep grazing on their thin acid soils.

North Herefordshire provides yet another change of rocks and consequent scenic variety. Here limestone and shales of the Silurian period, named by the geologist Sir Roderick Murchison after the Silures people who lived here in Romano-British times, form a series of scarps and vales centred on the Vale of Wigmore. The area is bounded by two beautiful rivers, Teme and Lugg, both equally prized by artists and anglers, and a sequence of steep-sided, heavily wooded valleys gives leisurely drives and walks in quiet seclusion. Forestry dominates much of the landscape, the habitat of a large population of deer, most readily seen in winter and spring when grazing tempts them out of the woodlands.

Herefordshire has been fortunate: it has escaped the ravages of the industrial revolution and thus its agricultural character has survived virtually intact. Today the soft rural environment provides one of England's most welcoming and unhurried holiday areas, a land to savour at leisure and then return to, time and again, an effective antidote to life in more hectic and less attractive parts of Britain.

2
The countryside

'The beautiful land is a gift from God' was the motto of the former Herefordshire County Council and natural beauty does indeed abound on all sides. The locations described in this chapter provide for all tastes; strenuous hikes across rugged uplands, bracing walks over rolling hills, leisurely strolls by rivers and through woods, or just a quiet picnic in beautiful surroundings. In addition, two long-distance footpaths cross Herefordshire: Offa's Dyke Path and the Wye Valley Walk, and also described here is the Teme Valley Leisure Drive.

Aymestrey Gorge, Aymestrey (map reference 137, 148, 149: 425654). 6 miles (10 km) north-west of Leominster, where A4110 crosses the river Lugg. Park on the riverside track behind the Crown inn.

The track leads upstream with the swiftly flowing Lugg on the right and the tree-covered side of the gorge rising almost vertically on the left. About 100 yards (90 metres) along, a steep bramble-strewn path leads off left up to the line of an abandoned quarry face, which provided much of the stone for buildings in the area. Visitors interested in seeing impressive cliffs of Aymestry Limestone will find the short climb amply rewards the effort. The main track continues along the gorge, hugging the edge of the forested area, often high above the river. The whole gorge is a panorama of ever changing views in a peaceful corner of Herefordshire. Wild flowers abound in spring and early summer, fungi in autumn.

Bircher Common (map reference 137, 148, 149: 465662). 5 miles (8 km) north-west of Leominster. A minor road leads up to the common from B4362. Once over the cattle grid, bear right and park on the roadside verge. National Trust.

From here you can walk in any direction: the lower slopes are bracken and gorse, giving way to open grassland as you climb higher. The upper area is Oaker Coppice, a delightful wood of mixed broadleaf and conifers intersected by tracks. Higher up, the views southwards across Herefordshire are more extensive. Adjacent to the western boundary of the common are extensive tracts of Forestry Commission woodland leading to Fishpool Valley and Croft Ambrey, both National Trust areas (see separate entries in this chapter).

Bradnor Hill (map reference 148: 698551). The approach is along a minor road leaving B4335 at 303570. This is near the roundabout on the Kington bypass, A44. Follow the minor road steeply upwards, over a cattle grid and past a golf club car park. Continue along this track until reaching a National Trust sign prohibiting further driving; cars may be parked here and there is bracing walking in every direction. National Trust.

If you continue along the track on foot, bearing left round the upper contours of the hill, there are superb views westward to the Welsh border country. The steep slopes of Stanner Rocks (see below) rise sharply across the valley, followed, as you continue round the hill, by Hanter Hill and Hergest Ridge (see below). The southern side of the hill gives a splendid panorama of Kington and the lower countryside southwards across Herefordshire to the Black Mountains.

Bringsty Common and Brockhampton Woodland Walk (map reference 149 : 694549). Park on the unsurfaced lay-by on A44 3 miles (5 km) east of Bromyard, on the edge of Bringsty Common. Woodland walk is National Trust.

Follow the path along the wall of Brockhampton Park to a gate giving access to the circular woodland walks amongst a variety of trees including great mature oaks. Adjacent to the park is Bringsty Common, a large undulating area of bracken and sheep grazing with good walks and views.

Bromyard Downs (map reference 149: 670553). 2 miles (3 km) east of Bromyard, approached on a minor road leading off either A44 (at 678544) or B4203 (at 670560) Partly National Trust.

This steeply sloping area is a mixture of common land and woods, giving pleasant walking and good views westwards towards the Welsh uplands.

Croft Ambrey (map reference 137, 148, 149: 444668). 6 miles (9 km) north-west of Leominster. National Trust.

This magnificent hillfort can be approached only on foot. Park outside Croft Castle (chapter 6) at 452655, then follow the signposted route through the park and on upwards through Forestry Commission plantations until you reach the ramparts of the fort. Walk round the ramparts for superb views in all directions, especially northwards across the Vale of Wigmore. An alternative return route leads down through Fishpool Valley (see below).

Dinedor Hill (map reference 149: 523364). 3 miles (4 km) south of Hereford. Hereford City Council.

This large hillfort (chapter 3) provides

pleasant walking under large broadleaf trees. A minor road leads steeply up to the entrance: turn left along the base of the rampart and continue until a wider area outside a youth camping area gives room to turn and park. The top of the rampart gives an excellent panoramic view northwards across the city of Hereford.

Fishpool Valley (map reference 137, 148, 149: 459656). 5 miles (7 km) north-west of Leominster, adjacent to Bircher Common and Croft Ambrey (see above). National Trust.

This valley cuts deeply into the heavily wooded hillside north of Croft Castle (chapter 6). Access to the lower end of the valley is to the right of the main drive leading up to the castle, shortly after crossing the cattle grid. There is limited parking at the edge of the drive; otherwise continue to the parking area at the castle gate. The series of fishpools are important aquatic habitats, partly designated a Site of Special Scientific Interest. At the head of the valley the walk can be continued upwards through Forestry Commission plantations to Croft Ambrey (see above).

Haugh Wood (map reference 149: 595365). This extensive woodland area lies in hilly land 6 miles (9 km) south-east of Hereford and is approached by a minor road leading up from Mordiford on B4224. Forestry Commission and National Trust.

Haugh Wood occupies the central area of the uplands known to geologists as the Woolhope Dome. Halfway through the wood there is a car park and picnic area with information board, leaflets and waymarked paths. A narrow strip of woodland either side of the minor road is ancient and owned by the National Trust. Immediately east of Haugh Wood is the wide expanse of Broadmoor Common, for those who prefer their picnics in open countryside.

Hay Bluff (map reference 161: 244366). Park beside the Gospel Pass road along the base of the hill.

At 2219 feet (677 m) Hay Bluff is not the highest peak of the Black Mountains but is the most accessible. From the road strike uphill, a stiff climb but safe enough in reasonable weather. The views in all directions are superb. Do not venture upwards in poor weather and take care of young children in the rougher upper section of the slope. See also Offa's Dyke Path below.

Herefordshire Beacon, Malvern Hills (map reference 150: 760400). Car park beside the A449 at 764403.

At 1115 feet (340 m), Herefordshire Beacon provides an exhilerating climb and magnificent views. Paths upwards from the car park. The Beacon can be included in a general walking day on the Malvern Hills (see below) or with a walk of some 2 miles (3 km) to Midsummer Hill (760375), which, like Herefordshire Beacon, is a hillfort (see chapter 4).

Hergest Ridge, Kington (map reference 148: 255563).

A long bracken-covered eminence on the border of England and Wales, Hergest Ridge is most easily reached from a minor road starting by Kington church (290567). Proceed as far along this road as practicable by car then park somewhere unobtrusive and continue on foot. On clear days there is an unrivalled panoramic view encompassing all Herefordshire and beyond. See also Offa's Dyke Path below.

Malvern Hills. East of Ledbury, crossed by A449.

The distinctive outline of this dramatic range is visible from far and near, providing splendid easy walking and memorable views in all directions. Paths run the whole length of

Herefordshire Beacon in the Malvern Hills.

the ridge from North Hill (150: 770465) to Hollybush Hill (150: 760365) some 6 miles (10 km) as the crow flies, but double that by the footpaths. The B4232 is a delightful scenic drive or walk from West Malvern (150: 764460) to Wynds Point (150: 764403) and there are numerous car parks along the way. Wyche Cutting (150: 770436) is a rock-hewn pass through to Worcestershire giving excellent views eastwards across the neighbouring part of the county. See also separate entries for Herefordshire Beacon and Midsummer Hill.

Marches Forest (map reference 148, 149: 495742). On the minor road from Wigmore to Ludlow. Forestry Commission. Here there is a Forestry Commission district office and car park. Various trails are marked out through forested landscapes in an area which supports a population of some five hundred fallow deer, including the rare long-coated variety. Leaflets on the trails and forest are available at the office. There is also a geological trail, mainly along the road, from 471729 to the A49 junction at 513741, tracing the rock succession in the area known as the Wigmore anticline.

Mary Knoll Valley (map reference 148, 149: 500720).

Park under the trees at the bend in B4361 2 miles (3 km) south-west of Ludlow. Forestry Commission. This delightful wooded area is part of Marches Forest. The path leads up the steep-sided valley beside a small stream which, for a short distance, forms the Herefordshire-Shropshire border. Various other paths and tracks lead off and you may wander more or less at will, encountering both broadleaf and coniferous plantations as you explore.

Midsummer Hill, Malvern Hills (map reference 150: 760375). A car park on A438 at 150: 762369 gives access to the hill. National Trust.

The hill is crowned by a hillfort (see chapter 3). The eastern flank of the hill is heavily wooded and there is a pleasant minor road running along the base which provides a shaded walk in high summer. Two huge quarries cut into the north and south sides of the hill expose the complicated geology of the Malverns. The car park also serves as a starting point for walking on Hollybush Hill (150: 760365), another National Trust holding immediately south of the road.

Offa's Dyke Path

The path does not follow Offa's Dyke: at times it coincides with or crosses it, just as it does the present Welsh-English border. Path, dyke and border follow independent courses from north to south, sometimes meeting, sometimes miles apart. Walking the path requires some planning: the appropriate Ordnance Survey maps, a good guidebook and, for upland sections, a compass and proper clothing are all necessities. Detailed planning can be undertaken with the aid of the Offa's Dyke Association, West Street, Knighton, Powys; telephone Knighton (0547) 528753. The description here is confined to three sections of the path falling within the area covered by this book.

Kington to Rushock Hill. Start at Kington market place (148: 295568), from the top corner, and follow the sign down across Back Brook and the bypass, then uphill steeply, past the golf club house on the right. The path keeps Bradnor Hill on the left, then branches sharp right above The Bower Farm (148: 291588) to join a section of the Dyke on Rushock Hill.

Kington to Hergest Ridge. Leave the market place at the lower end, turning right up the street towards the church. The road bears left and right around the church. Then take a left turn towards Hergest Croft Gardens (see chapter 6). The way now lies directly ahead, deteriorating from road to track and finally path as it climbs steadily to Hergest Ridge.

Both these walks give comfortable hill walking with superb extensive views. The Black Mountains section below is a different proposition, not to be treated lightly and to be avoided in any kind of bad weather. It is the most strenuous section of the entire path.

The Black Mountains. Take the minor road leading south from Hay-on-Wye towards Gospel Pass and park just beyond a junction at 161: 241376. The path climbs steeply up to Hay Bluff, 2219 feet (677 metres), and then follows the Welsh-English border all along the ridge between the Vale of Ewyas and the Olchon Valley. The going is undulating, rough and often wet and bitterly windswept, but the views on clear days are tremendous.

Olchon Valley (map reference 161: 288326). In the Black Mountains near Longtown.

Park on the small track and strike upwards in steep ascent of the ridge leading to Black Hill (161: 274348). Now bear left to the head of the valley and follow the steep course of Olchon Brook down past Blaen-Olchon Farm to the road and back to the car. This is a strenuous walk, not for young children and not to be attempted in poor weather. There are also two picnic sites on the opposite side of the valley.

Queens Wood, Dinmore Hill (map reference 149: 506514). On the A49, midway between Hereford and Leominster.

This countryside park occupying the summit

At Symonds Yat the Wye curves in a great loop against the northern cliffs of the Forest of Dean, providing some of England's most famous views.

of Dinmore Hill has a large car park, information centre, cafe and waymarked walks through mature woodland, including an arboretum of specimen trees. There are extensive views southwards from the lookout known as the toposcope. The considerable deer population is rarely seen in daytime, when there are large numbers of visitors (and their dogs).

Stanner Rocks (map reference 148: 263583). Beside the A44 3 miles (4 km) west of Kington.

Just over the Welsh border, these volcanic tree-clad cliffs rise dramatically beside the A44. Park on the wide verge and follow a track leading to the right past the base of the cliffs. After about 300 yards (275 metres), strike left up the steep, heavily wooded hillside until you reach a path running along a high contour. Turn left until the path emerges on the summit of the rocks. This is fairly rough walking and likely to be arduous for young children and impracticable for less active adults.

Symonds Yat Rock (Map reference 162: 563160). 6 miles (8 km) south of Ross-on-Wye. Forestry Commission.

One of England's famed beauty spots, the area immediately around Symonds Yat Rock becomes extremely congested during the summer. Symonds Yat Rock is high above a dramatic meander of the Wye. There are an extensive car park, refreshment cabin and information facilities. Waymarked woodland walks lead off in various directions, this being the northern extremity of the Forest of Dean. In the Wye Valley far below are the twin villages of Symonds Yat East and West on opposite banks of the river (chapter 7 and 11). See also Wye Valley Walk below.

Teme Valley Leisure Drive

This drive has been devised and signposted by the regional tourist board; a leaflet with a very clear map is available from Bromyard tourist information office (chapter 12). The circular route of some 50 miles (80 km) starts from Bromyard and encompasses a large area of the attractive hilly countryside of north-east Herefordshire, extending into corners of neighbouring Worcestershire and Shropshire. Noted for its orchards, the Teme Valley is particularly enjoyable when the spring blossom is in full flower; many of the hedges contain semi-wild fruit trees, particularly damson.

Westhope Hill (map reference 148, 149: 466522). 5 miles (8 km) south-west of Leominster.

This is open common located on upland,

commanding extensive views northwards. The area gives good walking and picnic sites. It can be approached most easily from the hamlet of Bush Bank on A4110, by the minor road which winds steeply up through the attractive hamlet of Westhope. An alternative access is from the A49 through the village of Hope under Dinmore, on the north side of Dinmore Hill.

Wye Valley Walk

This walk extends from Hay-on-Wye to Chepstow. The section from Hereford to Chepstow, is 52 miles (84 km), of which over half is in Herefordshire. A very useful plastic wallet is widely available containing practical information accompanying 1:50,000 Ordnance Survey map extracts. Although many sections of the walk follow the river bank, it also deviates to cut off large meanders and to follow footpaths through the delightful landscapes encountered. The route is waymarked. There are a number of points where the footpath crosses public roads and cars may be parked.

1. The walk starts at the corner of Castle Green, Hereford (149: 513395), where steps descend to Mill Street (limited parking), so use the car park south of the old Wye Bridge (149: 509395), walk downstream to the suspension footbridge and cross to the starting point.
2. Bunch of Carrots inn, Hampton Bishop (149: 549382).
3. Mordiford Bridge (149: 570374).
4. How Caple (149: 603303).
5. Hole-in-the-Wall (149: 611286).
6. Ross-on-Wye: riverside car park (162: 593240).
7. Goodrich: Kerne Bridge (162: 581192).
8. Symonds Yat East (162: 560158). This section is very congested in summer.

There are no more access points within Herefordshire: the next convenient point is Monmouth Bridge.

Roman mosaic floors from Magna, at Kenchester, 5 miles (8 km) west of Hereford, are displayed in Hereford City Museum.

Man's earliest monument in Herefordshire: Arthur's Stone is on a remote ridge above Dorstone.

3
Places of archaeological interest

The earliest settlers in Herefordshire apparently moved up the Wye Valley and sheltered under cliffs and in the mouths of caves. Several thousand years later, neolithic man left his mark on about twenty sites in Herefordshire, mainly in the form of barrows and standing stones. By the time of the iron age, however, the area was well peopled: there are about thirty well defined hillforts and camps. Almost all sites are on private land: this chapter describes five forts with public access and where a visit is rewarding for the extent of the remains and the dramatic views.

Some fifteen sites show signs of Roman settlement, the most important being at Kenchester (137/149/161: 438428), Leintwardine (137/148: 404741) and Weston under Penyard (162: 645240), but none has evidence visible or readily accessible to the casual visitor. Herefordshire was crossed by a number of Roman roads, principally the north-south borderland road from Caerleon to Chester, via Kenchester and Wroxeter, usually called Watling Street West.

Kenchester, 5 miles (8 km) west of Hereford, was the town of *Magna,* some 22 acres (9 ha) in extent. Successive excavations have yielded mosaic floors, coins, pottery and jewellery. A selection, including the mosaics, are in Hereford City Museum. **Leintwardine,** 10 miles (14 km) north-west of Leominster, was the fort of *Bravonium,* probably a supply base for the advance garrisons further west in Wales, while at **Weston under Penyard,** 3 miles (5 km) east of Ross-on-Wye, was the settlement of *Ariconium,* where, besides coins and other artefacts, excavations have revealed furnaces, clay pits and other indications of a substantial industrial site, associated with iron ore workings in the Forest of Dean.

Visitors wishing to research more extensively should seek assistance at the Hereford City Museum and Library, where the Transactions of the Woolhope Club can be consulted and finds and maps are displayed.

Arthur's Stone, Dorstone (map reference 161: 318431). English Heritage.

On a high windswept site between Dorstone and Bredwardine, this megalithic tomb of the neolithic period stands beside a minor road. The stones have fallen or toppled from their original positions but the momument remains impressive. The largest stone is estimated to weigh 25 tons.

Capler Camp, Fownhope (map reference 149:593329).

This is a double-rampart iron age fort

perched high above a broad sweep of the river Wye 1 mile (1.6 km) south-east of Fownhope, in Capler Wood. Park where the Wye Valley Walk runs up through the wood at 592324: the path is clearly marked leading steadily up-ward, until emerging on the open southern ramparts of the fort.

Croft Ambrey hillfort (map reference 137,149: 444668).

Three main building phases have been identified in this iron age hillfort, the total enclosed area being some 24 acres (9.5 ha). Excavations led to an estimate of a settlement comprising some three hundred small four-post buildings, the site being occupied for perhaps six hundred years before the Roman conquest. Numerous artefacts, including iron tools, weapons and pottery, are in Hereford City Museum. For access directions see entry in chapter 2.

Dinedor Camp, Dinedor (map reference 149: 523364).

A single rampart and ditch surround the site of an iron age fort of about 10 acres (4 ha), an original entrance being preserved at the east-ern end. It is easily approached by car: for access directions see under Dinedor Hill in chapter 2.

Hereford defences, Mill Street, Hereford.

A viewing platform gives permanent access to excavations showing four successive stages from the ninth century Saxon palisade and rampart to the massive thirteenth-century stone wall. Restored bastion and wall can be seen above Greyfriars Bridge.

Herefordshire Beacon, Malvern Hills (map reference 150: 760401).

Only a visit can do justice to the spectacular site of this iron age hillfort and the views from this second highest point on the Malvern Hills. The bare, windswept outline of the ramparts is seen in silhouette from a considerable dis-tance. The enclosed area of some 20 acres (8 ha) is elongated, following the winding summit ridge. Traces of many hut hollows can be seen. The highest point was converted into a medieval castle mound. For access directions see chapter 2.

King Arthur's Cave (map reference 162: 546155) and **Merlin's Cave** (map reference 162: 548152), Whitchurch.

Located in woodland above the gorge sec-tion of the Wye Valley near Seven Sisters rocks, downstream from Symonds Yat, these two caves need perseverance to find and great care when entered. Amateurs should not attempt to explore them. King Arthur's Cave has yielded by far the greater number of finds, indicating occupation, either continuously or intermittently, from upper palaeolithic to bronze age times (some nine thousand years). Bones of animals typical of early postglacial conditions have also been recovered, including hyena, cave bear and woolly rhinoceros. Finds can be seen in Hereford City Museum.

Midsummer Hill, Malvern Hills (map refer-ence 150: 760375).

Located towards the southern end of the Malvern Hills, 2 miles (3 km) south of Here-fordshire Beacon, the area enclosed by this iron age hillfort is about 20 acres (8 ha), protected by a single rampart and ditch with two entrances. Excavations indicated around five centuries of continuous pre-Roman occupation in about 250 buildings. For access directions see chapter 2.

Offa's Dyke

Unlike neighbouring Powys, Herefordshire contains only short identifiable stretches of this great Saxon earthwork. Offa ruled Mercia from AD 757 to 796 and the Dyke is generally attributed to the later years of his reign, after the last Welsh raid of 784. The purpose of the Dyke remains unclear, but practical considera-tions indicate that its primary function would have been as a border delineation, and poss-ibly a check on cross-border travel, rather than defensive. Regardless of purpose, the Dyke represents a formidable engineering and logis-tical achievement, an indication of the power and organisation of the Mercian kingdom in the late eighth century.

The best area to search is east of Kington, at 148: 329559, south-west of Lyonshall church, and at 148: 322577, on the east bank of the river Arrow (where the embankments of a disused railway may be confused with the Dyke).

Visitors wishing to investigate the Dyke seriously must cross the border to Knighton, in Powys, and visit the Offa's Dyke Centre, in West Street; telephone Knighton (0547) 528753. See also chapter 2, Offa's Dyke Path.

Rowe Ditch

This less prominent earthwork straddles the Arrow valley just west of Pembridge: from the A44 at 148/149: 382578 northwards to the minor road at 148/149: 379604. It can be most easily seen in its middle section, from the minor road west of Leen Farm at 148/149: 380593. Again, the purpose of this construc-tion is uncertain: it lies 4 miles (5 km) east of the section of Offa's Dyke near Lyonshall church, mentioned above, and may have represented an earlier attempt at boundary definition, or a local cross-valley defence against the frequent Welsh incursions before 784.

The impressive ruins of Goodrich Castle, which was besieged and captured by Parliamentary forces in the Civil War.

4
Castles and monastic ruins

Like all counties of the Welsh Marches, Herefordshire was studded with castles of varying degrees of strength. Careful perusal of the Ordnance Survey maps will reveal many moated sites from which the buildings have long since disappeared. Hereford once had one of the greatest castles of the realm, but not one stone now remains: only the earthworks bear testament to its former strength. Goodrich Castle alone retains enough of its structure to demonstrate the role these fortresses played in holding a resentful local population in check and the neighbouring Welsh at bay. There remain, however, a number of sites worth visiting for their extensive earthworks and attractive locations. This section lists the most accessible.

CASTLES
Clifford Castle, Clifford HR3 5EU (map reference 148, 161: 244456). Telephone: Clifford (049 73) 230.

On a dramatic eminence high above the river Wye 2 miles (3 km) north-east of Hay-on-Wye, parts of the gatehouse, hall and twin towers remain on a steep motte. Clifford Castle was the home of Jane Clifford, Henry II's mistress, known as 'Fair Rosamund' (see

chapter 10). It was destroyed by Owain Glyndwr in 1402. The castle is on privately owned land, but access may be obtained at reasonable times on application to Mr and Mrs Parkinson at the house by the gate.

Goodrich Castle, Goodrich, Ross-on-Wye (map reference 162: 577199). English Heritage.

4 miles (6 km) south of Ross-on-Wye and sited on a prominent bluff overlooking two former fording places of the river Wye, the castle, the best preserved in the county, retains much of its stonework and provides good views of the surrounding countryside. The earliest record of 'Godric's Castle' is of 1102, and the twelfth-century square keep is the oldest part. During the Civil War, Sir Henry Lingen held the castle for the Royalists until King Charles surrendered. Following a siege of six weeks, during which the castle was bombarded by the mortar 'Roaring Meg' (now on show in Churchill Gardens, Hereford), Parliamentarian forces under Colonel John Birch (see Weobley church, chapter 5) captured the castle and a long period of decline began. An information centre, picnic site and other facilities are provided.

Castle Green, Hereford.

Hereford Castle site, Castle Green, Hereford (map reference 149: 513396).

Castle Green, beside the river south-east of the cathedral, was the site of one of the first Norman castles in England. Some appreciation of the extent of the defended area of this important royal castle can be gained by walking around the top of the broad embankments. The keep was razed in 1645 and the stone subsequently sold for building. Castle Pool, on the north side, is part of the former moat. The site was landscaped in Victorian times.

Kilpeck Castle, Kilpeck (map reference 149, 161: 443306).

These well preserved motte and bailey earthworks lie 8 miles (11 km) south-west of Hereford adjacent to Kilpeck church (see chapter 5). The layout of the kidney-shaped bailey and circular motte is clearly discernible; two ruined sections of a polygonal keep of considerable size survive. There are views all round and across to the Black Mountains. The grouping of castle, church and village make a very satisfying monument to post-conquest settlement.

Longtown Castle, Longtown (map reference 161: 320291).

Longtown, 5 miles (8 km) west of Pontrilas, is dominated by its castle on the site of a Roman fort on a prominent spur where the rivers Olchon, Monnow and Escley join. The keep of the thirteenth- and fourteenth-century castle may have been the earliest round keep in England. Some masonry survives and there is free access at any reasonable time.

Pembridge Castle, Welsh Newton (map reference 162: 488193). Telephone: Skenfrith (060 084) 226.

This castle is not at the village of Pembridge but a mile west of the hamlet of Welsh Newton, which is on A466, 3 miles (4 km) north of Monmouth. It is a fortified manor house of the fourteenth century, built on the site of a thirteenth-century castle. It is still lived in and not open to the public, although visitors may walk round the outside of the building on Thursdays from May to September. From here the aged Catholic priest John Kemble (see chapter 10) was taken to be hanged in Hereford in 1678.

Snodhill Castle, Snodhill (map reference 161: 323404).

Good masonry remains on a prominent spur above the Golden Valley, 1 mile (1.6 km) south-east of Dorstone. The earthworks extend over 10 acres (4 ha). It is a steep but short climb up through the bailey to the impressive twelfth-century keep but there are some rewarding views of the outer hills of the northern Black Mountains.

Stapleton Castle, Stapleton, near Presteigne, Powys (map reference 137,148: 323655).

The ruins occupy a prominent hilltop site 1 mile (1.6 km) north-east of Presteigne, just inside the Herefordshire border with Wales. A stile at the road junction at the base of the hill gives access to a short but vigorous scramble up to the ruins. Delightful all-round views of neighbouring hills and valleys make this an ideal place for a summer picnic. Little is known of this remote castle, but the ruins are those of a seventeenth-century house on the earlier castle site.

Weobley Castle site, Weobley (map reference 148,149: 403514).

As at Hereford, the impressive earthworks provide a popular recreation space but nothing remains of the stonework. Shaded by huge chestnut trees, this is another delightful summer picnic spot. See also under Weobley in chapter 11.

Wigmore Castle, Wigmore (map reference 137,148: 408693).

The gaunt, sadly neglected ruins of this stronghold of the Mortimers, Earls of March, look down over the village of Wigmore 10 miles (16 km) north-west of Leominster. From the main village crossroads, take the road leading up past the church until your way is barred by a farm gate. On a bank to the right is a stile. Walk across the sloping field and find one of the various ways through the overgrown ruins to the summit. The views of the surrounding scarplands are superb. In the middle ages great tournaments were held at the castle when the King's Council met there.

Wilton Castle, Ross-on-Wye (map reference 162: 591244).

By Wilton Bridge, just west of Ross-on-Wye, the castle has no public access but is plainly visible from the bridge or the riverside footpath. It was built to defend a ford but was ruined in the Civil War.

MONASTIC RUINS

As with castles, Herefordshire contains no monuments of the first rank. There are, however, a number of sites well worth a visit for their delightful settings as well as their remaining stonework.

Abbey Dore (map reference 149,161: 386303).

A Cistercian abbey was established here in 1147. Of the large complex of monastic buildings of the late twelfth and thirteenth centuries the chancel and transepts survive. The present tower was built in the seventeenth century. The soaring height of the interior is impressive but much of the masonry is in poor condition. Some restoration was undertaken in the seventeenth century, when the flat ceilings and Jacobean screen were installed by John Abel (see chapter 10) for Lord Scudamore. The magnificent screen surmounted by a huge coat of arms is best viewed from the wooden

Pembridge Castle is a superbly preserved border fortress.

Jacobean gallery facing it. Notice also the wall paintings and inscriptions, unfortunately partly faded and obliterated. In the choir ambulatory there are many fragments of Norman masonry, including carved stone bosses, recovered from the now destroyed monastic buildings.

Blackfriars Monastery, Widemarsh Street, Hereford (map reference 149: 512404).

In Widemarsh Street, some 400 yards (365 metres) north of the city centre, and located in a pleasant public garden, are the remains of this early fourteenth-century foundation, expelled from within the city confines by Bishop Cantilupe after quarrels between the monastery and the cathedral authorities. Ruins of the refectory and cloisters remain but the most interesting feature is the preaching cross, which most unusually survives almost intact, although much restored. A visit should be combined with one to the adjacent St John and Coningsby Medieval Museum (see chapter 7).

Craswall Priory, (map reference 161: 272377).

Only three houses of the Grandmontine Order were founded in England and Craswall is by far the best preserved. Set beside a small tributary of the River Monnow in a remote

The soaring arches of ruined Llanthony Abbey.

Black Mountains valley, the priory did not attract the attention of stone robbers after falling into decay. Founded around 1225, the priory was occupied for a little over two centuries until being abandoned in 1441. The remains are cared for by a volunteer group, Craswall Grandmontine Society: further information can be obtained from the City of Hereford Archaeology Committee's offices at Hereford Town Hall.

Dinmore Preceptory, Dinmore Manor, near Hereford (map reference 148,149: 485503).

The scant remains of this preceptory of the Knights of St John of Jerusalem are in the grounds of Dinmore Manor (see chapter 6).

Flanesford Priory, Kerne Bridge, near Ross-on-Wye (map reference 162: 579194).

The refectory of this Augustinian priory, dating from 1346, stands in fields on the bank of the Wye near Kerne Bridge, south of Goodrich Castle. It has been converted into holiday flats. At Kerne Bridge (1828), one of the best nineteenth-century bridges in this area, may be seen the last of the Wye coracles and coracle makers.

Leominster Priory, Leominster (map reference 148,149: 498594).

Adjacent to the Priory Church (see chapter 5), the nave of the original Norman church survives as the northernmost of the three parallel naves of the church. Of the remainder, only a few fragments survive, with a range which may have been the infirmary, partly rebuilt after the Dissolution. Leominster was an ancient religious foundation: a nunnery in Saxon times, dissolved in 1046, preceded the Benedictine foundation given by Henry I to the newly founded Reading Abbey in 1123.

Limebrook Priory, Lingen (map reference 137,148: 374661).

A mile south of Lingen, by a sharp right-angled turn between two ancient houses on a minor road, only a fragment remains of the early thirteenth-century nunnery where six nuns and their attendant community lived until the Dissolution in 1539. It is worth calling this way for the remote beauty of this little valley of Limebrook, one of the unvisited corners of Herefordshire.

Llanthony Abbey, Llanthony (map reference 161: 288278).

The wonderful ruins, just over the border in Gwent, are second only to Tintern in this area, and the site is more beautiful. Deep in the Vale of Ewyas which cuts into the Black Mountains, this is a place of peace and contentment. An ancient church is adjacent to the ruins, and there is a fine old inn nearby.

Hereford Cathedral from Wye Bridge.

5
Churches and chapels

Herefordshire has dozens of village churches which repay a visit and many have leaflets explaining the main points of architectural and historical interest. Any selection must be somewhat arbitrary: this chapter indicates some of the churches generally regarded as of special interest; others are mentioned under particular villages (chapter 11) or in the context of other chapters. Dedicated village church visitors will find still more for themselves, by studying the Ordnance Survey maps and following the winding byroads of Herefordshire.

Aymestrey: St John and St Alkmund.

Located in the narrow pass from the Vale of Arrow to the Vale of Wigmore, the church occupies a delightful setting against the steep slope of School Wood, 6 miles (9 km) northwest of Leominster. The carved sixteenth-century screens across the chancel and two side chapels are exceptional.

Bacton: St Faith.

This remote little church overlooking the Golden Valley is notable for its monument to Blanche Parry, Maid of Honour to Queen Elizabeth I. The figures are extraordinary: a large Blanche Parry in profile kneeling before an oddly truncated queen facing forwards. The lengthy inscription with its idiosyncratic Elizabethan spelling takes patience to decipher.

Bredwardine: St Andrew.

The church is splendidly situated high above the river Wye 12 miles (18 km) west of Hereford. Francis Kilvert (see chapter 10) was rector here for the final two years of his life, 1877-9. A lot of Norman work survives, including much of the south doorway, the font and carvings. There are fourteenth- and fifteenth-century effigies of knights. The church is approached along a tree-lined avenue and there is a good riverside walk downstream across the site of Bredwardine Castle.

Brinsop: St George.

This little church in a valley 5 miles (7 km) north-west of Hereford is packed with interest, not least for its associations with William Wordsworth, who stayed at nearby Brinsop Court several times, an association commemorated by stained glass windows. There is much fine Norman sculpture, intricate and intriguing, including a carving of St George on a large tympanum. This saint is also depicted in the east window. The oak chancel screen, heavily restored but originally fourteenth-century, is simple but impressive.

Brockhampton (near Ross-on-Wye): All Saints.

A thatched curiosity of 1902, this church by W. R. Lethaby is set in a soft, garden-like churchyard ringed with evergreen shrubs, approached through a thatched lych gate. More house than church in proportions, the building sits happily in its setting. Inside, in perfect proportion, the pointed arches plunge dramatically to shoulder height. Notice the use of concrete for the vaulting of the chancel and transepts and the delicately carved flower motifs on the choir stalls, repeated in sensitive embroidery on several pew cushions. A tapestry depicting two angels was designed by Burne-Jones. Across the road a neo-Jacobean lodge serves as the village post office.

Burrington: St George.

Tucked away in the wooded hills 3 miles (5 km) north-east of Wigmore, this little church is remarkable for its row of six massive cast iron slab tombstones, set in the ground outside the east wall of the church. Dated from 1619 to 1678 and embossed with coats of arms and splendid lettering, most of them are monuments to the Knight family (see chapter 10). Opposite is the Victorian Picturesque former school and further up the lane are a number of timber-framed houses.

Garway: St Michael.

Remotely situated almost on the Welsh border, in the Monnow valley, 5 miles (8 km) south-east of Pontrilas, this is a fascinating little church with an early thirteenth-century tower joined by a passage to a corner of the nave. The excavated remains of a rare round nave can be seen: in the late twelfth century this was a preceptory of the Knights Templars, the round nave being a copy of the church of the Holy Sepulchre in Jerusalem. Nearby is a huge circular dovecote of 1326, part of the religious foundation and well worth visiting. The massive walls, 4 feet (1.2 metres) thick, contain 666 nesting alcoves; a hole in the domed roof gave access for the doves.

Hereford: Cathedral Church of St Mary the Virgin and St Ethelbert the King. Telephone: Hereford (0432) 59880.

This is one of the twenty-six great cathedrals of the realm. Records start with Bishop Putta (AD 676) but the present building was begun shortly after the Conquest, about 1080. A fine and varied selection of Norman work survives, followed by examples of work from all succeeding architectural periods. During your visit make sure you see: Bishop Audley's Chantry, a two-storey Tudor (1500) addition to the south side of the Lady Chapel; *Mappa Mundi,* a unique allegorical world map of about 1300 in the north choir aisle; the Treasury in the Crypt under the Lady Chapel (see chapter 7); and the Chained Library, by far the largest in the world, together with the Muniment Room with some thirty thousand documents dating from the Anglo-Saxon period onwards (see chapter 7).

Conducted tours of the great tower are given and provide an unforgettable experience. The first stage of the ascent is by a stone stairway concealed in one corner of the high-ceilinged north transept. A walkway across the upper side of this ceiling shows how the whole structure, tons of masonry, is supported by a central row of great keystones. Similar views along the nave and south transept are also obtained from a high-level gallery around the great tower. Further ascents lead to the bellringers' chamber, the bells themselves and finally out on to the roof of the tower. This is Hereford's unrivalled viewpoint, looking down over the whole city spread out on either side of the Wye.

Outside the main building visit the Vicars' Cloister, Chapter House garden (toilets), Bishop's Cloister (shop and refreshments) and Song School and Library.

Hereford: All Saints.

At the opposite end of Broad Street from the Cathedral, this church contains a chained library of some three hundred volumes, nearly sold to an American in about 1900, and which can be seen by appointment. Dating from around 1290, the building had to be buttressed on the north side in the early nineteenth century, having developed a serious tilt as it was built on the line of an early ditch. The subsequent twist to the spire is a noted city landmark. The choir stalls with their misericords are excellent examples of fourteenth-century wood carving. On the east wall is a fine wall painting showing part of a large kneeling figure.

Hereford: St Peter.

There are canopied choir stalls of the fifteenth century in the huge chancel, 60 feet (18 metres) long. On 27th March 1085 Walter de Lacy, founder of the church, fell to his death from the battlements of the former tower during a tour of inspection.

Hoarwithy: St Catherine.

This extraordinary south Italian Romanesque village church 8 miles (11 km) south of Hereford, perched high above the Wye and

Kilpeck has one of England's best small Norman churches, with a famous decorated doorway.

the attractive village of Hoarwirthy, was built by J. P. Seddon in the second half of the nineteenth century. The square four-storeyed campanile appears to be the outstanding architectural feature until the external south cloister walk is seen. Noteworthy internal features are the Byzantine east end with four massive Devonshire marble columns, the neo-Romanesque capitals of many of the columns, the arch of doves, the mosaic floor and the stained glass, which portrays ten saints.

Kilpeck: St Mary and St David.

Located 7 miles (11 km) south-west of Hereford, this is one of England's finest small Norman churches, especially renowned for its Norman sculpture of the Herefordshire school. Pure Norman, the church has nave, chancel and apse with no later additions. From the wooden gallery one can appreciate the overall sturdiness of the interior. Examine particularly the chancel arch pillars, each with three carved saints. Outside there is wonderfully intricate carving around the south doorway and an extraordinary array of decorated corbels running at eaves level right round the building: animals, heads and figures in wonderful profusion, a few removed by prudish Victorians for the indelicacy of their subject matter and lost for ever. The site appears to be pre-Norman: the churchyard is a raised, almost circular, enclosed area, typical of the *llan*, or Celtic religious site. See also Kilpeck Castle, chapter 4.

Ledbury: St Michael and All Angels.

This is probably Herefordshire's finest parish church: its long nave and flanking aisles with their tall piers soar to almost cathedral proportions. There is a wealth of monuments, spanning several centuries, including one to the father of Elizabeth Barrett Browning, and a striking copy by T. Ballard of Leonardo's 'Last Supper' above the altar; another version hangs over the north porch entrance. The north chapel, impressive by any standards, is high and light, its tall windows embellished with hundreds of ballflower ornaments. Outside, the majestic detached bell tower rises 200 feet (60 metres) from its massive base.

Leominster: Priory Church of St Peter and St Paul.

Shorn of its monastic buildings at the Dissolution and further devastated by fire in 1699, the church is unusual in appearance, more so because there are three parallel naves of the twelfth, thirteenth and fourteenth centuries. The north nave, the original priory church, is Norman, supported on columns that would grace any cathedral. The central nave has a superb west window, 45 feet (14 metres) tall and richly traceried. The equally lofty south nave reflects the town's prosperity in the fourteenth century when its high-quality wool, 'Lemster ore', was famed throughout the land. A hundred years later Henry V's longbowmen at Agincourt were dressed in tunics of Lemster ore, if Shakespeare is to be believed. A curiosity is the folding ducking stool, complete with wheels, last used for two local scolds in 1807 and 1809.

Much Marcle: St Bartholemew.
Notwithstanding its fine architecture, it is the glorious monuments which put Much Marcle on the list of churches not to be missed in Herefordshire. First, at the western end of the nave, is the rare painted oak figure of Walter de Helyon, a fourteenth-century yeoman. Next, in the north wall of the chancel, is the ornate memorial to a lady generally assumed to be Blanche Mortimer, Lady Grandison, who died in 1347: note particularly the skilful way in which the mason draped a fold of the skirt down over the base of the tomb. Above is another, much later (early seventeenth-century) monument, to Elizabeth Boughton, portrayed kneeling at her prayer desk.

These lead us to the great glory of Marcle church: the two tombs and the many wall monuments in the north chapel. In the northwest corner are a late fourteenth-century couple. Fine though these effigies are, they are surpassed by the superb seventeenth-century marble figures of Sir John and Lady Kyrle, representing the height of the mason's art: the painstaking accuracy of every fold, every feature, every tiny detail is extraordinary. One is left in awe of the skill and devotion of a craftsman able to produce such work.

In the churchyard, flanked by ranks of ancient tombstones, is the great Marcle yew, with a seat inside its cloven trunk for seven people, its great boughs supported by a framework of props. The church stands by the entrance to Homme House, which is not open to the public, but over the way is the drive to Hellens, which is open (see chapter 6).

Pembridge: St Mary.
Located 7 miles (11 km) west of Leominster, Pembridge was formerly a market town and decayed medieval borough and has an appropriately large and well furnished church, but it is the bell tower that remains in most people's minds. Completely detached from the main building, the tower is a sturdy three-stage pagoda-type structure, similar to the stave churches of Norway. Inside are the massive oak braces and beams; eight huge posts support the strucutre, each simply a squared-off oak-tree trunk. An ambulatory gives access all round the interior of the tower and a view of the intricate workings of the clock.

Peterchurch: St Peter.
In the heart of the Golden Valley, 12 miles (17 km) west of Hereford, stands this majestic church of abbey-like proportions, its Norman interior almost perfectly preserved, and unusual in having two chancels. The sequence of three great rounded arches decreasing in size

In Much Marcle church the superb Kyrle monument is a tribute to seventeenth-century stonemasonry.

At Pembridge the detached bell tower is structurally similar to the stave churches of Norway.

and leading the eye to the single lancet window in the apse, is most impressive. Outside the river Dore hurries alongside the churchyard and the new spire stands out starkly against the stone the Normans quarried.

Ross-on-Wye: St Mary.

Splendidly situated on a cliff of Old Red Sandstone high above a sweeping loop of the Wye, at the highest point of the town, this is a town church of impressive proportions, although much restored. Numerous architectural features will detain the seasoned church visitor but it is the profusion and sumptuous quality of the monuments that is most memorable. Chief among these are the tombs of the Rudhall family, whose fortunes were founded by William Rudhall, Attorney General to Henry VIII. Also notable is the monument to John Kyrle, Man of Ross (see chapter 10). Outside is a plague cross dated 1637 and recording 315 burials.

Shobdon: St John Evangelist.

Shobdon church, 7 miles (11 km) north-west of Leominster, is unlikely to be forgotten. Its park-like setting and conventional exterior contrast with the visual fantasy within. Here is Strawberry Hill Gothick at its most sumptuous, an architectural extravaganza in Wedg-wood blue and white, like a giant wedding cake. The south transept was the Bateman family pew, comfortably furnished and warmed by a large fireplace: opposite, in the north transept, the servants' pew has strictly utilitarian furnishings and no fireplace.

The remains of the old church survive as Shobdon Arches, an estate folly along a tree-lined grass avenue leading north from the church, now sadly eroded by two centuries of exposure to the elements. A replica of the present church, complete in every detail, was erected in 1986 on the ranch of a millionaire film producer in Virginia.

Tyberton: St Mary.

This large red-brick church of 1721 is prominently sited on B4352 8 miles (12 km) west of Hereford. Its spacious interior contains a number of notable features: box pews; a whole series of marble tablets to the Brydges family, dating from 1668 to 1793; several fine painted coats of arms in the bellringers' chamber; a good font, lectern and reredos. Most impressive of all, however, is the panelling by J. Wood of Bath, completed in 1731, of the internal apsidal east end. It is rich in impeccably carved emblems.

The setting is interesting, attractive and odd. The churchyard is surrounded by an

Vowchurch: St Bartholomew.

This is a delightful little church in a lovely setting on the bank of the river Dore. From the outside, the timber bell-tower rises from the apex of the nave roof: inside is some of the most impressive timber beamwork in Herefordshire. Looking upwards from the nave, the vista is of a great profusion of tie-beams and collar-beams, all supported on most unusual oak pillars soaring from floor to eaves, each a chamfered tree trunk. The nave and chancel are a structural entity, the only division being a Jacobean screen, with engagingly unsophisticated carvings of Adam and Eve, some pear-shaped (forbidden?) fruit and dragons. Across the churchyard is the timber-framed former vicarage with the timber struts of the gable in an unusual herringbone pattern. By the stone bridge across the Dore is a pretty picnic spot.

Weobley: St Peter and St Paul.

At the northern extremity of the famous village of Weobley, 11 miles (18 km) north-west of Hereford, the soaring spire on top of the massive fourteenth-century tower is visible for miles around. The tower is almost de-tached, just joined to the north-west corner of the nave, its upper profile most impressive with four tall pinnacles joined to the base of the spire by flying buttresses. Inside the outstanding feature is the uncompromising white marble statue of Colonel John Birch in armour. He was Herefordshire's most prominent supporter of the Parliamentary cause in the Civil War and became governor of Hereford Castle, owner of the Bishop's Palace and an MP.

unusual ha-ha: nearby is a timbered gatehouse leading on to the drive to Tyberton Court, but across the parkland, instead of the expected mansion, is a modern bungalow at the end of outbuildings and a walled garden. The Court, former seat of the Brydges family, has been demolished.

6
Historic houses and gardens

Herefordshire has a good representative sample of historic houses open to the public, besides examples of the landscaping of Lancelot 'Capability' Brown, Humphry Repton and the Picturesque designers. In the eighteenth and early nineteenth centuries Herefordshire became a leading area for exponents of Picturesque landscaping, in the estates of Richard Payne Knight at Downton and Sir Uvedale Price at Foxley.

Berrington Hall, Leominster. Telephone: Leominster (0568) 5721. Entrance on A49 3 miles (5 km) north of Leominster. National Trust.

Berrington Hall is Herefordshire's prime example of a Georgian country mansion. Commissioned by Thomas Harley of the prominent Harleys of Brampton Bryan, the grounds were laid out by Lancelot 'Capability' Brown and the house was designed by Brown's son-in-law Henry Holland junior, the fashionable Whig architect noted for Carlton House and numerous other well known buildings.

From the parkland the entrance is through a triumphal arch to the formal pleasure gardens, traversed by a long walk bordered by low clipped yews. A second arch between two stable blocks leads into a rear courtyard flanked by service blocks containing the laundry and dairy; the servants' hall is now a tea room and shop.

The drive curves round to the main entrance, the west front, a striking exercise in classical simplicity and perfect symmetry. The facade is dominated by a large decorated pediment supported on four slender Ionic columns soaring the full height of the building and forming an imposing portico for the front door. The ground floor has a series of delightful rooms, notable for their friezes, fireplaces, furniture, paintings and, especially, the decorated ceilings. Perhaps the finest ceilings are those in the Drawing Room, with its magnificent central medallion of Venus, Cupid and Jupiter, and the Library, with cleverly executed silhouettes of well known people painted flat but giving the impression of bas-relief. Occupying the centre of the house, the Staircase Hall rises the full height of the building to a glass-domed lantern, giving an airy, spacious atmosphere to the completely enclosed area. There is a gallery running around the hall at first-floor level with fine marble columns, cast iron balustrade and delicate statuettes in niches. Opening from this gallery are further rooms open to the public, including an enchanting nursery.

Burton Court, Eardisland, Leominster. Telephone: Pembridge (054 47) 231. Entrance on minor road 1 mile (1.6 km) south of Eardisland.

Berrington Hall is Herefordshire's finest Georgian mansion, the work of Henry Holland junior, who designed the Carlton Club and other London landmarks.

Sited prominently on a mound approached by a sweeping drive, the house is a mixture of styles, mainly Georgian but with Victorian additions and a double-storey entrance tower of 1912 by Sir Clough Williams-Ellis of Portmeirion fame. Together these styles make a pleasing combination, a good example of a country squire's seat rather than a stately home. Inside, the Great Hall is a remarkable survival from the original early fourteenth-century house, its tall roof supported by six pairs of collar-beams. Burton Court is noted for its comprehensive costume exhibition which occupies the Great Hall and several other ground-floor rooms, together with an exhibition of curios from all over the world.

Croft Castle, Yarpole, Leominster. Telephone: Yarpole (056 885) 246. Entrance off B4362 5 miles (8 km) north-west of Leominster. National Trust.

One of Englands oldest noble families, the Crofts, have been associated with this site since the reign of Edward the Confessor. Apart from a break from 1746 to 1923, Crofts have lived at Croft Castle for more than nine centuries. A long line of crusades, campaigns and high offices of state testifies to the family's sense of duty and there were members of Parliament in the family from 1296 to 1727. A cross-border alliance was created when John de Croft married one of Owain Glyndwr's daughters.

The fortunes of the family were frequently closely allied with their powerful neighbours the Mortimers of nearby Wigmore Castle (see chapter 4) and in 1461 the Battle of Mortimer's Cross (see chapter 7) was fought on Croft land. The victor, Edward Mortimer, Earl of March, was crowned Edward IV a month later. Sir Richard Croft provided both mounted and foot soldiers for the Yorkist cause in this battle and was also married to a member of the Mortimer family. With such credentials it is not surprising that Crofts served in high office during the Yorkist reigns. The close alliance with royalty proved less fortunate two hundred years later during the Civil War: the castle was plundered by discontented Irish mercenaries who had not been paid, members of the family were imprisoned or died in battle and the defences of the castle were demolished.

During the period when the Crofts were not in residence Croft Castle was occupied by the Knight and Johnes families, whose wealth derived from ironmaking in Shropshire and Worcestershire. Richard and Thomas Knight (see chapter 10) distinguished themselves in many fields of study.

The castle is approached by a magnificent avenue of beech and oak: on the right the ground drops steeply to Fishpool Valley (see chapter 2), the avenue ending at a late eighteenth-century Gothick curtain wall and gateway. Beyond this is a wide lawn, separated from the deer park by a ha-ha. Across the lawn is the pleasant little early fourteenth-century church of St Michael, with box pews and memorials to the Croft family. Particularly notable is the fine altar tomb of Sir Richard and Dame Eleanor Croft, a Mortimer widow who was governess to the ill-fated young sons of Edward IV.

Croft Castle is more house than castle, a roughly square building with a tower at each corner dating from the fourteenth or fifteenth century. A series of rooms filled with good furniture, books and pictures is open to the public. Much of the interior Gothick decoration dates from the eighteenth century and is the work of Thomas Farnolls Pritchard. The

Croft Castle has been the home of the Croft family since the early eleventh century.

The mock medieval splendour of Eastnor Castle: on the horizon is Herefordshire Beacon in the Malvern Hills, surmounted by an iron age hillfort.

Blue Room is particularly delightful; Jacobean panelling cleverly painted with gilded rosettes shadowed to give the impression of bas-relief lines the walls and there is a splendid early Georgian fireplace. There are extensive walks in the grounds, varying from a stroll in the formal gardens to a strenuous walk up to the iron age settlement at Croft Ambrey (see chapter 3).

Cwmmau Farmhouse, Brilley, Whitney on-Wye HR3 6JP. Telephone: Clifford (049 73) 251. 5 miles (8 km) south-west of Kington. National Trust.

This superb Jacobean timber-framed farmhouse survives virtually unaltered in an extremely remote location in hilly country. Opening is restricted to bank holiday weekends or by telephone appointment.

Dinmore Manor, Hereford. Telephone: Hereford (0432) 71322. 6 miles (10 km) north-west of Hereford.

A minor road leaves the A49 at 149: 502495, leading along the valley with the heavily heavily wooded southern slopes of Dinmore Hill crowding in on either side. Dinmore Manor is hidden deep in a secret place, its flower-laden garden carved out of a forested hillside and giving panoramic views across Herefordshire to the Malvern Hills. The Manor is enchanting, for its garden and setting and for its appealing mixture of architectural styles: several periods of building rest on medieval foundations, but the most striking features are the music room and cloisters (of 1929-36) which encompass one end of the garden. A chapel of the Knights Hospitaller of St John of Jerusalem, part of a large monastic foundation of 1189, stands in the garden. The music room, cloisters, gardens and chapel are open daily throughout the year.

Eastnor Castle, Eastnor, Ledbury HR8 1RN. Telephone: Ledbury (0531) 2302 or 2304. 2 miles (3 km) east of Ledbury; entrance in Eastnor village.

At first sight the castle, its turreted towers rising from the trees across the lake, appears to be a relic of the age of chivalry, a perfectly preserved medieval castle. But this is all an illusion: Eastnor Castle dates from 1812 when John, second Lord Somers, laid the first ornamental stone of a magnificent country seat which reflects the self-confident exhuberance of the early nineteenth-century landed families.

No expense was spared: Sir Robert Smirke, who had designed the British Museum and Covent Garden Theatre, was engaged as architect. Basic building stone was transported from the Forest of Dean by mule trains but the more decorative stones came from far and wide. The estate provided oak for floors, panelling and doors but large timbers for roofing supports were in short supply, the best being requisitioned for naval building. Undaunted, Smirke designed cast iron roof trusses, the first known departure from the use of timber for this purpose in a private house.

Fake castle though it is, Eastnor provides a sumptuous feast of magnificent rooms crowded with trophies, fine furniture and pictures. Apartments open include the entrance hall; the great hall, 60 feet (20 metres) long and 55 feet (18 metres) high, with a splendid collection of armour; the inner hall, with even finer armour; the dining room, with a fine painted ceiling in panels and a large collection of portraits; the Gothic Drawing Room, by Pugin, decorated in 1849 in the flamboyant style fashionable at the time; the octagonal salon; the sumptuous long library (63 feet or 21 metres) designed by Fox, lined with oak book-cases surmounted by magnificent Flemish tapestries; the little library; the staircase hall; the state bedroom and dressing room.

There are also the terraced gardens, extensive parklands and lakeside walks to enjoy and explore. On a nearby hillside across A438 a track leads to an obelisk (150: 753379) in memory of the eldest son of Lord Somers who was killed at Burgos in the Peninsular War.

This perfectly preserved octagonal dovecote is in the grounds of Hellens at Much Marcle.

South of this (150: 749373) are the ruins of Bronsil Castle, mid fifteenth-century, reached by a lane from A438. At the entrance to the castle grounds is the delightful nineteenth-century estate village of Eastnor (see chapter 11).

Hellens, Much Marcle, Ledbury HR8 2LY. Telephone: Much Marcle (053 184) 668. 4 miles (6 km) south-west of Ledbury on A449.

Substantially Jacobean, but with fragments of earlier periods, this is one of England's oldest family homes, originally founded in 1290 and lived in by the descendants of the same family ever since. The estate originated over two centuries earlier, in the immediate post-Conquest period, when it was one of the estates of the Marches, created to keep the Welsh at bay, and was held by a branch of the powerful Mortimer family. The house was at the centre of national intrigue when in 1326 Roger Mortimer fell in love with the French queen of Edward II and installed her at Hellens, protected by a private army. The subsequent well known imprisonment and murder of Edward at Berkeley Castle availed Roger Mortimer little: he was hanged for treason at Tyburn on the orders of Edward's son and successor. Today Hellens is a mellow brick building on the foundations of the former castle, with a number of rooms furnished with pictures, tapestries, armour and other family memorabilia. Outside there is a small terraced garden and an impressive octagonal Tudor brick dovecote erected by Fulke Walwyn in 1641. Opening times are restricted and should be checked by telephone or with tourist offices (chapter 12).

Kentchurch Court, Kentchurch, near Pontrilas, Hereford HR2 0DB. Telephone: Golden Valley (0981) 240228. The entrance is opposite Kentchurch church, 10 miles (16 km) south-west of Hereford.

Originally a late medieval castle, the present house is largely Nash's work of about 1800: only the gatehouse and lower portion of the massive tower survive from the earlier building. There are some extremely intricate wood carvings attributed to Grinling Gibbons, brought from Holme Lacy mansion, former seat of the Scudamores, together with pictures, furniture, porcelain and stained glass. Behind the house the fallow deer park rises to the 1100 foot (336 metres) summit of Garway Hill. The house is open during the summer months by telephoning Mrs J. Lucas-Scudamore on the stated number.

Lower Brockhampton, Bringsty, Worcester WR6 5UH. Telephone: Bromyard (0885) 88099. Entrance at Bromyard Lodge on A44, 2

Lower Brockhampton, in a remote valley near Bromyard, has a unique timbered gatehouse spanning the moat.

miles (3 km) east of Bromyard. National Trust.

Hidden in a remote wooded valley and approached by a long minor road, Lower Brockhampton is a delightful example of a medieval moated house. The hall and parlour are open but the chief delight is the fine timbered gatehouse spanning the moat. Across the farmyard are the ruins of a twelfth-century chapel. Nearby are Bromyard Downs and Bringsty Common (see chapter 2).

Moccas Court, Moccas, Hereford HR2 9LH. Telephone: (098 17) 381. Entrance off B4352, 10 miles (16 km) west of Hereford.

Moccas Court stands in a superb location in parkland on the bank of the river Wye. 'Capability' Brown and Humphry Repton laid out the grounds; Robert Adam and John Nash designed the house and lodges. There are a number of fine rooms including a circular drawing room facing the river. The oval hall rises the full height of the house to a large glazed dome. The house is open on Thursday afternoons in summer months. The adjacent church is largely Norman with a good tomb chest of a knight of the early fourteenth century.

Sufton Court, Mordiford, Hereford HR1 4LU. Telephone: Holme Lacy (043 273) 268. On a minor road just north of the village of Mordi-

ford 4 miles (6 km) east of Hereford.

A park by Humphry Repton, on sloping ground looking across the wide lowland where the Lugg meets the Wye, provides the setting for this attractive Palladian house designed by Wyatt in the 1780s and open for a restricted time each summer.

A short distance north, at 149: 575384, is Old Sufton, undergoing reconstruction. It shows stages of development from a single-storeyed manor house to a nineteenth-century farmhouse. There are remains of a 'painted room' of about 1450 and a Celtic coffin lid can be seen outside on the chimney breast. There is a fine circular brick dovecote of the eighteenth century, surmounted by a large lantern. Beside Old Sufton are extremely impressive quarried exposures of the local rock on this western flank of the Woolhope Hills.

GARDENS AND GROUNDS

These gardens and grounds of privately owned houses are open on a regular basis but none of the houses is open. Current times can be checked at tourist offices (see chapter 12) or by telephoning the number included in each entry.

Abbey Dore Court Garden, Abbey Dore, Hereford HR2 0AD. Telephone: Golden Valley (0981) 240419. 12 miles (17 km) south-west of Hereford.

The swiftly flowing waters of the little river Dore hurry through this tranquil garden, located at the lower end of the Golden Valley. Broad lawns, herbaceous borders and soaring Wellingtonia give variety on the east bank, linked by a footbridge to the rockpool garden and an open view across the valley to Abbey Dore (see chapter 4). There is also a walled garden with a sales area for plants. In the seventeenth-century stables refreshments are served. A small Jersey herd provides rich cream.

Bosbury Vineyards and Gardens, The Slatch, Bosbury, Ledbury HR8 1JS. Telephone: Bosbury (053 186) 226. 3 miles (5 km) north of Ledbury.

Here there are large vineyards and gardens with specimen trees and shrubs and water features providing a habitat for ornamental waterfowl and geese. A sixteenth-century timber-framed oast house has been converted into a buffet room. It is open by appointment only for groups of twenty to sixty.

Broadfield Court Vineyards, Bodenham. Telephone: Bodenham (056 884) 483. 10 miles (16 km) north of Hereford.

Tours of the vineyards and gardens and wine tasting can be arranged by appointment only.

Brobury Garden and Gallery, Brobury, Hereford HR3 6BS. Telephone: Moccas (098 17) 229.

This riverside garden is magnificently situated on the cliff-like bank of the river Wye beside the six-arched eighteenth-century Bredwardine Bridge, Herefordshire's finest and earliest brick-built bridge. Brobury House, built in the 1880s in the manner of a Scottish hunting lodge, is surrounded by 8 acres (3 ha) of beautifully kept gardens encompassing herbaceous borders, specimen shrub areas, fish pools, a bridge and pond, all overlooked by mature specimen oaks, copper beech, lime and conifers. Wheelchair access is possible on gravel paths around all parts of the garden, with seats at regular intervals to enjoy the views. Across the river stand Kilvert's Vicarage (see chapter 10) and Bredwardine church (see chapter 5). An art gallery adjacent to the house sells topographical prints, maps and watercolours of every county of the United Kingdom.

Hergest Croft Gardens, Kington HR5 3EG. Telephone: Kington (0544) 230218. Entrance along a minor road just west of Kington church.

There are three separate gardens, the largest occupying a beautiful wooded valley, lush with superb rhododendrons and azaleas. In addition there are Edwardian and old-fashioned kitchen gardens near the house, with plants for sale. Nearby are Hergest Ridge, Bradnor Hill and Stanner Rocks, all fine walking country (see chapter 2).

Horseway Herb Garden, Horseway Head, Staunton-on-Arrow, Leominster HR6 9HS. Telephone: Pembridge (054 47) 212.

Tucked away in a remote little valley west of the village of Staunton-on-Arrow, this cottage garden is packed with the heavily scented herbs of traditional cuisine and medicine, many available for sale, together with recipe sheets.

Stoke Lacy Herb Garden, Stoke Lacy, Bromyard HR7 4JH. Telephone: Hereford (0432) 820232. On A465, 4 miles (6 km) south-west of Bromyard.

This is a small herb nursery and garden with a wide variety of herbs. It is open on Saturdays only from May to September.

The Weir, Swainshill, Hereford. On A438, 6 miles (9 km) west of Hereford. National Trust.

This superb spring garden on a steeply sloping bank of the river Wye, with cliff garden walks, is open at advertised times from Easter onwards.

Museums and other places of interest

HEREFORD

The city is well endowed with museums and other places of interest to the visitor. A free leaflet giving opening times, brief details and a map is available from the Tourist Information Centre (see chapter 12). Those in the city centre are included in the perambulation of Hereford in chapter 11: the others, in outer areas of the city, all have car parks.

Bulmer Railway Centre, Whitecross Road, Hereford HR4 0LE. Telephone: Hereford (0432) 274378.

Staffed by volunteers and therefore open only at weekends, the centre was established in 1968 to house the *King George V,* the former Great Western locomotive number 6000, after its rescue from obscurity and restoration by H. P. Bulmer. It carries a bell on the buffer beam, a memento of its visit to the United States in 1927 to celebrate the anniversary of the Baltimore and Ohio Railroad Company. Two other locomotives are also based here; *Princess Elizabeth* (London Midland and Scottish, 6201) and *Clan Line* (Southern, 35028) as well as industrial locomotives and rolling stock. Steam days and special events are held during each season.

Churchill Gardens Museum and Hatton Gallery, 3 Venns Lane, Hereford HR1 1DE. Telephone: Hereford (0432) 267409.

The museum occupies a substantial house on the summit of the south-facing slope of Aylestone Hill, 1 mile (1.6 km) north of the city centre. From its terrace there is a fine panorama of the city. A pleasant public park stretches away down the slope. On the terrace is the deadly mortar 'Roaring Meg' used to awesome effect in the siege of Goodrich Castle (see chapter 4). The museum contains costumes, furniture and paintings of the eighteenth and nineteenth centuries, a corn dolly room and various other period rooms. A corridor leads to the Hatton Gallery (1973), a fitting memorial to the local artist Brian Hatton, who was killed in the First World War.

Hereford Cathedral Chained Library, Hereford Cathedral, Hereford HR1 2NG. Telephone: Hereford (0432) 58403.

The best example of its kind in the world, this wonderful collection contains nearly 1500 books chained to cases dating from 1611. There are 227 manuscript volumes, the earliest being an eighth-century copy of the Four Gospels and the latest a copy of Wycliffe's translation of the Bible, known as 'The Cider Bible', of about 1420. There are 92 manuscripts of the twelfth century. The hundreds of printed books include two works printed by Caxton. The Cathedral Library also has many hundreds of unchained books and the Muniment Room houses some thirty thousand documents dating from early medieval times.

Hereford Cathedral Treasury, Hereford Cathedral, Hereford HR1 2NG. Telephone: Hereford (0432) 59880.

Housed in the crypt are the chalices, patens and other valuable relics from the cathedral and from many other churches throughout the diocese. The crypt itself is also architecturally interesting, being the last crypt to be built in an English Cathedral, around 1220: the style is, therefore, graceful Early English rather than the heavy Norman columns and arches common to all other crypts. The altar and reredos (1920) are a First World War memorial.

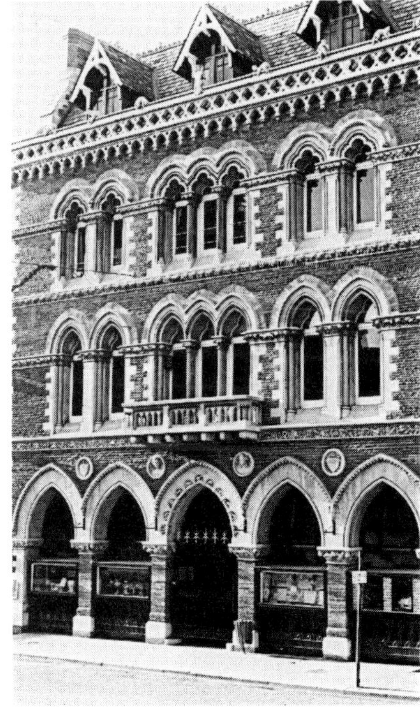

Hereford City Museum.

The former Great Western locomotive number 6000, 'King George V', is based at Bulmer Railway Centre in Hereford and is licensed for main line working.

Hereford City Museum and Art Gallery, Broad Street, Hereford HR4 9AU. Telephone: Hereford (0432) 268121, extension 207.

In the porch is a circular relief map of Herefordshire, excellent for gaining a visual impression of the geography of the county. Upstairs the museum records the archaeology, history and natural history of the district in a series of interesting display cases. Beekeeping is featured in an observation hive. Adjoining is the art gallery, with exhibitions that are changed each month. Downstairs is the Reference Library, including the very comprehensive local collections.

Herefordshire Regimental Museum, Harold Street, Hereford. Telephone: Hereford (0432) 272914.

The relics of the former county regiment, colours, uniforms, equipment, weapons and photographs, are displayed, together with the flag and pennant of Grand Admiral Doenitz, last Führer of the Third Reich. Other colours and drums of the regiment occupy a place of honour in the Town Hall: see below. Check opening arrangements before visiting.

Herefordshire Waterworks Museum, Broomy Hill, Hereford. Telephone: Hereford (0432) 57411. 1 mile south-west of the city centre.

The mid nineteenth-century pumping station for the city houses an excellent collection of working exhibits with a regular programme of steaming days for both engines and boiler. Broomy Hill looks out across the Wye and there is a nineteenth-century water tower at the top, in the grounds of the modern waterworks.

Museum of Cider, The Cider Mills, 21 Ryelands Street, Hereford HR4 0LW. Telephone: Hereford (0432) 54207.

The museum is devoted entirely to the

history of cidermaking and is housed in a redundant early section of the H. P. Bulmer factory, now the world's largest cider producers. Employing modern display techniques, the museum relates the history of cidermaking through the ages and presents a series of impressive exhibits including a huge seventeenth-century French beam press, a reconstructed nineteenth-century farm cider house, hydraulic presses from the 1920s and a whole series of early cider-manufacturing processes. Some of the exhibits had been used for farm cidermaking for up to three centuries before being presented to the museum.

At the King Offa distillery cider brandy is being produced for the first time in Britain for many years: it was common in the sixteenth and seventeenth centuries but declined due to heavy taxation. A great 40 gallon (182 litre) copper pot still of 1905 is in the museum, brought from a farm at Calvados in Normandy by Mr Bertram Bulmer and restored to working order. Two distilling processes produce 1 gallon (4.5 litres) of brandy from 40 gallons (182 litres) of cider: the maturing process in oak casks takes three years. Her Majesty the Queen presented an oak from Windsor Great Park to provide the casks.

The Old House, High Town, Hereford. Telephone: Hereford (0432) 268121, extension 224.

An outstanding example of a Jacobean town house, built in 1621, the Old House is three storeys high and timber-framed. It is the only surviving building of the former Butchers Row, which was demolished in the nineteenth century. The whole house is open to the public as part of the City Museum and contains furniture and domestic effects of the seventeenth century, including four-poster beds.

St John and Coningsby Medieval Museum, Widemarsh Street, Hereford HR4 9HN. Telephone: Hereford (0432) 272837.

Full of surprises, this delightful museum is part of a hospital founded by Sir Thomas Coningsby in 1614. It is housed in the former dining hall and infirmary and incorporates an adjoining chapel. Armour, models of pensioners in hospital uniforms and the skeleton of a fifteenth-century abbot in a floor tomb are amongst the exhibits. This is the site of an older foundation, probably dating from the reign of Richard I as the Hospital of St John of Jerusalem. It was presented by the king to the Commandery of St John at Dinmore Manor (see chapters 4 and 6).

Emerging through the quadrangle of six stone almshouses an arch leads into neighbouring Blackfriars Garden. Here are the ruins of the Monastery of Friars Preachers, also called Dominicans or Blackfriars; a preaching cross survives in a remarkable state of preservation. Car parking is available on the southern side of this beautiful rose garden.

The Shire Hall, St Peter's Square, Hereford. Telephone: Hereford (0432) 272395.

The centre of local government before Herefordshire was merged with Worcestershire, the Shire Hall is imposing both outside and in. Completed in 1819, the front facade is classical Greek, a large pediment supported by eight tall Doric columns. Inside, the lofty grand corridor leads to a raised assembly hall, added in 1862. On either side of the corridor are two excellent panelled courtrooms; that on the right also served as the Herefordshire County Council Chamber. Downstairs, under the courtroom, is a range of nineteenth-century cells. The Shire Hall was designed by Sir Robert Smirke, a leading architect of the early nineteenth century, who also designed the British Museum. The statue of Sir George Cornewall Lewis MP in the forecourt is by Baron Marochetti (1864).

The Town Hall, St Owen Street, Hereford. Telephone: Hereford (0432) 268121.

Completed in 1904, this provides a pleasing contrast to the Shire Hall on the opposite side of the road, in both style and colour. The style is complicated, with polygonal towers, a deeply arched canopy and balcony over the entrance and a lantern tower surmounting the roof. The brown terracotta contrasts with the very light grey of the Shire Hall. Inside, the entrance hall is sumptuous with an imposing divided staircase leading up to the first-floor assembly hall and council chamber. Downstairs, in a strongroom, are the city plate and charters, which can usually be viewed on application to the custodian. These are the finest treasurers Hereford has to show. The Town Hall was designed by H. A. Cheers.

LEDBURY
Both these small museums are in Church Lane, the cobbled medieval alley leading up to the church: see Ledbury, chapter 11.

Butcher Row House, Church Lane, Ledbury. Telephone Ledbury (0531) 4534.

This timber-framed house has been moved twice; originally one of a row of sixteenth-century shops that ran down the centre of the High Street, it was re-erected behind 14 High Street, then moved to its present position and restored by Ledbury and District Society. The remainder of the row was demolished in 1830 in a town improvement plan. The museum displays a miscellaneous collection of local bygones and papers: the building is a good example of a jettied town house. Behind Butcher Row House is Burgage Hall, the former Congregational chapel, renovated for the use of the townspeople.

Ledbury Heritage Centre, Church Lane, Ledbury. Telephone: Ledbury (0531) 2461.

The late fifteenth- or early sixteenth-century timber-framed building was originally a meeting place, possibly a guildhall, with a market place on the ground floor. It subsequently became a grammar school until 1837, when it fell into disuse. A number of different uses followed including, according to unverified accounts, a pin factory, a drill hall for the local rifle volunteers, workhouse workshops and a reading room. By 1969 the building was vacant and the District Council undertook its restoration, opening it as a Heritage Centre in 1978. Information and displays are provided on the construction and development of the building itself and on the growth of Ledbury from an Anglo-Saxon village to modern market town.

LEOMINSTER
Leominster Folk Museum, Etnam Street, Leominster. Telephone Leominster (0568) 5186 or 2520.

This voluntarily run museum displays a wide

Mortimer's Cross monument.

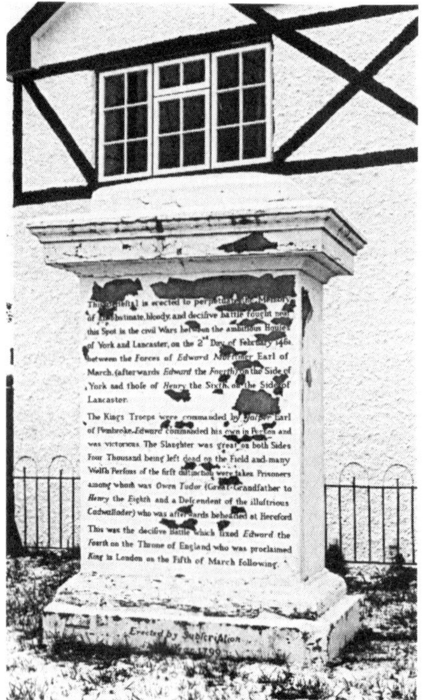

range of artefacts relating to the archaeology and agricultural history of the area, with costumes, maps and old photographs of Leominster.

MORTIMER'S CROSS
Battlefield site (map reference 137, 148, 149: 425636).

Mortimer's Cross is not a village, simply a public house, toll house and a few cottages grouped around a crossroads on A4110, 5 miles (8 km) north-west of Leominster.

It is notable for being the site of the Battle of Mortimer's Cross on 3rd February 1461, the bloodiest day in Herefordshire's history. To view the site, park in the lay-by on B4362 immediately east of the road junction. Stand facing across the road with the bridge over the Lugg to your left. The wide field stretching before you, part of the Great West Field of the village of Kingsland, is where most of the conflict took place. The battle occupies a significant place in English history, as it was the decisive one that led to the culmination of the Wars of the Roses and the establishment of the Yorkist line on the throne.

The opposing forces were led by the leading warriors of the day. Jasper Tudor, Earl of Pembroke, commanded the Lancastrian force, a cosmopolitan army of Welsh, French and Bretons, supported by the Earl of Ormond with his Irish contingent and the elderly Owen Tudor, Jasper's father. Opposing them was Edward, Earl of March, eldest son of the Duke of York and a member of the powerful Mortimer family. A morning of bitter and murderous conflict left Edward the victor; a month later he was acclaimed King Edward IV in London, still only nineteen years old: the crown of England had been won in a remote Herefordshire field.

See also the two painted signs outside the Mortimer's Cross Inn and the monument (1799) 1 mile (1.6 km) south on the A4110 outside the Monument Inn, which details the day's events.

Mortimer's Cross Mill, Lucton. English Heritage.

The watermill is open only on Thursday afternoons. In use until the 1940s, it is in full working order and provides a complete demonstration of the gravity feed method used to operate these mills, once common on all main Herefordshire rivers.

SYMONDS YAT WEST
A complex of visitor services and attractions will be found here, catering for the huge numbers drawn to Symonds Yat and the surrounding area by its dramatic natural beauty: see also Symonds Yat Rock (chapter 2) and Symonds Yat East and West (chapter 11). The

The chain ferry at Symond's Yat.

complex is located off the A40 at Whitchurch interchange (162: 552175), along B4164 on the bank of the river Wye. Here you will find catering facilities, souvenir shops, boat trips, an interpretative centre (Countryside Commission), waymarked walks, craft workshops, garden centre and the riverside church of St Dubricius. The visitor centre telephone number is Symonds Yat (0600) 890360. Nearby are several other attractions.

Herefordshire Rural Heritage Museum, Great Doward, Symonds Yat, Ross-on-Wye HR9 6DZ. Telephone: Symonds Yat (0600) 890474.

This is one of the largest collections of farm machinery, vintage tractors, antique engines and rural bygones in Britain. There are some fifty tractors, dating from 1917 to the 1950s, a varied collection of horse-drawn wagons and implements and hundreds of domestic items. The collection is accommodated in a series of nine sheds.

Jubilee Maze, Symonds Yat West, Ross-on-Wye HR9 6BY. Telephone: Symonds Yat (0600) 890360.

Created to mark Queen Elizabeth II's Silver Jubilee in 1977, this is a traditional hedge maze set in a beautiful country garden. At the entrance visitors are welcomed by a maze man clad in Victorian boater and blazer, inspired by Jerome K. Jerome's *Three Men in a Boat.* The entrance garden was laid out by Julian Dowle, Chelsea Gold Medallist, who also designed the Jubilee Garden at Rotorua in New Zealand, that city's tribute to the Silver Jubilee. There are twelve different routes to the Temple of Diana in the centre, a viewing gallery from which to direct members of your family who are hopelessly lost and a Museum of Mazes and Labyrinths which traces their history from early pagan times. There are illuminated evening openings during the summer season.

Symonds Yat Bird Park, Symonds Yat West, Ross-on-Wye. Telephone: Symonds Yat (0600) 890989.

Opened in 1985, the bird park houses some 160 species from throughout the world, ranging from tiny nectar feeders to exotic parrots. There is a collection of ornamental park birds and pheasants and the aviaries and flights are laid out in a garden setting. Particularly engaging are the tame parrots which will sit on visitors' shoulders for photographic sessions.

World of Butterflies, Wye Valley Visitor Centre, Whitchurch, Ross-on-Wye HR9 6DA. Telephone: Symonds Yat (0600) 890655.

A wide variety of free-flying butterflies can be seen in a tropical environment created by landscaped pools, unusual plants and winding pathways.

WEOBLEY
Museum of the Weobley Historical Society, Back Lane, Weobley. Telephone: Weobley (0544) 318353.

This small museum is normally open on summer weekends.

8
Cider

History of cider

Herefordshire has long been associated with cider. The beginnings of the drink are lost in prehistory: long before the Romans arrived the apple and its attendant mistletoe were sacred, and the Celts are thought to have worshipped an apple god. Through the centuries cider was drunk in castle, manor house and farmstead throughout the county, made from the infinite variety of apples in orchards on every farm. A book published in the early seventeenth century, *Herefordshire Orchards, a Pattern for All England,* extolled the virtues of the county's cider and its promotion was undertaken by Lord Scudamore and other wealthy landowners. The diarist John Evelyn said of Herefordshire: 'in a manner it hath become one continuous orchard.'

War with the French first favoured the cider industry; it was a substitute for imported wine during the Hundred Years War in the fifteenth century. Four hundred years later, when Napoleon's blockade forced up the price of grain, many orchards were grubbed up to provide more profitable arable land. Thus began a period of decline throughout the nineteenth century, when cider became an essentially local drink, with very little exported to other parts of Britain. Almost every farmhouse would nevertheless have pressed some cider to supply the local labour force and, perhaps, one or two of the many cider public houses dotted about each parish.

Cider production was rescued from the doldrums in 1887 by Percy Bulmer, a son of

Cider once formed part of the wages of many farm workers.

the Rector of Credenhill, near Hereford. In that Golden Jubilee year he first pressed apples from the vicarage orchard and laid the foundations for the modern cider industry.

Cider apples

Originally a wild fruit, gathered by the Celts from the forests, the cider apple is small and bitter. At one time there were some 365 varieties known, with such eccentric names as Slack-my-Girdle, Skyrme's Kerne, Handsome Maud's and many others. Inevitably some have disappeared, but enthusiasts keep at least a hundred varieties thriving in specialist orchards dedicated to preserving the best of the traditional strains.

Cidermaking

Traditionally cider was pressed by means of an animal or person operating a beam connected to a large stone wheel, which ran round a circular stone trough to crush the apples. Heavy screw presses extracted the juice. Remains of these old cider mills can be found in numerous public locations and private gardens throughout the county.

The modern cider industry was born when Percy Bulmer moved into Hereford in 1888, bought apples from local farmers and made 4000 gallons (18,000 litres). From then on the firm was expanding almost continuously. A breakthrough came with the control of the fermentation process by the isolation of pure cider yeast: hitherto the wild yeast had rendered fermentation unpredictable and large-scale production hazardous. Each of the stages of production became mechanised as increasing quantities of apples had to be processed. The harvest begins arriving in mid September and, in a heavy year, may last until Christmas, when some 50,000 tons of apples will have been delivered.

After being tipped into silos for washing, the apples are milled to pulp to extract the juice, which is settled in vats. From here it is pumped to a vast undergound storage cavern containing 120 oak vats, the largest holding 60,000 gallons (272,760 litres). Yeast is added and the fermentation process of four to twelve weeks begins.

Storage is on an enormous scale. Originally 100 gallon (455 litre) oak casks sufficed and these increased steadily to 60,000 gallons (272,760 litres). Glass was used after the First World War created a shortage of oak: it lined 100,000 gallon (454,600 litre) rectangular tanks. In 1954 came the first steel tank, with a capacity of over half a million gallons (2,273,000 litres). By 1975 Hereford had the

monster 'Strongbow' tank holding 1.6 million gallons (7,273,600 litres), the largest container for alcoholic liquid in the world! West of the city centre, these tanks dominate the landscape, storing between them 15 million gallons (68,190,000 litres) of cider.

PLACES TO VISIT

The Museum of Cider in Hereford should be visited by anyone interested in the history and techniques of cidermaking: see the entry in chapter 7. In addition, there are four independent producers whose premises can be visited: Dunkertons at Pembridge, Knights at Storridge, Symonds at Stoke Lacy and Westons at Much Marcle. The first two are relative newcomers run by husband and wife teams; Symonds and Westons are much larger companies, the two survivors, apart from Bulmers, of a number of cider producers which formerly existed in Herefordshire. Both are still operated by members of the respective families, as is Bulmers: cider is still very much a family business in Herefordshire. Tours of Bulmers factory are normally available only to organised parties and need to be booked well in advance. Contact H. P. Bulmer Holdings plc, Cider Mills, Plough Lane, Hereford HR4 0LE.

The four cider companies listed here all have retail sales facilities (with tasting) and limited visiting arrangements. Opening hours and visiting should be checked by telephone.

Dunkertons Cider Company, Luntley, Pembridge, Leominster HR6 9ED. Telephone: Pembridge (054 47) 653. Located on a minor road 2 miles (3 km) due south of Pembridge.

Ivor and Susie Dunkerton started cidermarking in 1982 in order to help recompense for the loss of local farmhouse cider. Specialities include strong, still, full-bodied ciders and perry which can be tasted straight from the oak casks. Only genuine cider apples such as Foxwhelp, Sherrington Norman and Yarlington Mill are used, some being unique to the

LEFT: *Millions of apples arrive at the Hereford plant of H. P. Bulmer each autumn.*

RIGHT: *Cider matures in massive oak vats in a storage area of cathedral-like dimensions.*

Pembridge area. Fruit is brought in between September and January from local farms and orchards and the varieties are kept separate during pressing and fermentation: no water is added. Blending for balanced flavour and character takes place at regular intervals throughout the year. The blended ciders then mature until ready for drinking in oak casks named Adam and Eve.

Knight's Cider, Crumpton Oaks Farm, Storridge, near Malvern, Worcestershire WR13 5HP. Telephone: Malvern (068 45) 4594. Just off the A4103 at Storridge on the Hereford to Worcester road.

Knights Crumpton Oaks farm cider is made from local apples, different from those of the Pembridge area and therefore producing a different cider range from Dunkertons, dry, medium and sweet, all produced by traditional methods.

Symonds Cider and English Wine Company Ltd, Cider Mills and Winery, Stoke Lacy, Bromyard HR7 4HG. Telephone: Munderfield (088 53) 411. On A465 at Stoke Lacy,

midway between Hereford and Bromyard.

The Symonds tradition in cidermaking dates back to 1727, when William Symonds MD first made cider from his orchard. The company expanded dramatically in 1984 with the installation of a new cider mill and production plant. The wide range of ciders, including the strong traditional 'Scrumpy Jack', are made from English cider apples and in addition perry, English wine, fruit wine and fruit juices are produced. There is a company shop where products can be sampled and pre-arranged tours for visitors are conducted.

H. Weston and Sons Ltd, The Bounds, Much Marcle, Ledbury HR8 2NQ. Telephone: Much Marcle (053 184) 233. On A449 Ledbury to Ross-on-Wye road.

This is another family firm, established in 1880, producing 2 million gallons (9 million litres) of cider and perry annually. A wide variety of apples is used and the firm produces a correspondingly varied range of ciders and perry including special vintage brands and traditional scrumpy. There is a shop, tasting facilities and tours.

A county calendar

There are a number of events held between May and October which provide enjoyment for visitors as well as local people. All those listed are well advertised in the local press and further information can be obtained from the tourist information centres (chapter 12).

The **Three Choirs Festival** is Europe's oldest musical festival, dating from around 1720 and an event of international standing. There is a three-yearly rotation of venue between Worcester (1987), Hereford (1988) and Gloucester (1989) and so on, with the cathedral in each city providing the main focus, but with an increasingly varied and lively fringe programme being developed in recent years. Since the late nineteenth century, the Festival has been linked with Sir Edward Elgar (see chapter 10) and his works. The Festival lasts for a week in the middle of August.

May
River Wye Raft Race: May Bank Holiday. A three-day 100 mile (161 km) race from Hay-on-Wye to Chepstow, this is the world's longest and most gruelling event of its kind and the subject of intense competition among the more serious crews. There are many viewpoints from banks and bridges.

Hereford May Fair: second week in May. Henry I granted Bishop Richard de Capella a charter to hold a fair in the city each year about the time of the feast of St Ethelbert. During the three days of the fair the city centre is closed to traffic. At the opening ceremony the Mayor presents the Bishop with 12½ bushels of wheat, using an ancient bushel measure from the City Museum. The Mayor receives a free ride on the dodgems.

Herefordshire Music Festival, Hereford. Competitive and of a high standard.

Hereford Regatta: on the Wye, late May Bank Holiday.

June
Kington Festival and Eisteddfod.
Vale of Arrow Trotting Races, Kington.
Hereford and West of England Rose Show: late June. An event of national standing: the society was formed in 1867, the forerunner of the Royal National Rose Society, also

A champion Hereford.

conceived in Hereford, and now the world's largest specialist flower society.

July

Bromyard Gala. A two-day event featuring steam, crafts, horticulture and arena events. There are splendid parades of vintage steam locomotives and a traditional funfair.

Madley Festival. Highly rated for its top-class musicians and range of programme.

August

Herefordshire Country Fair. Traditional country field sports, dog show and demonstrations, crafts. The venue changes annually.

Herefordshire and Border Counties Aero Model Rally. A wide range of working and flying models, and numerous additional attractions. A two-day rally, in the grounds of Eastnor Castle, near Ledbury (chapter 6).

Leominster Show and Ledbury Carnival: late August Bank Holiday.

September

Kington Show and Kington Horse Show.

Bromyard Folk Festival, one of the country's premier events for lovers of traditional music and dance, with many fringe events.

Pembridge Art and Craft Market. Work by many local artists may be purchased. The art is hung in the school hall; the ancient market house (see under Pembridge, chapter 11) contains the craft stalls.

Ladies' Raft Race, on the Wye from Bridge Sollars to Ross-on-Wye, over the central section of the May course. A two-day event, just as demanding and just as keenly fought.

October

Hereford Antiques Fayre.
Ledbury Hop Fair.

The Three Counties Show is usually held in the second week of June. It used to rotate between the three counties of Herefordshire, Worcestershire and Gloucestershire, like the Three Choirs Festival, but now there is a permanent showground at Malvern, just east of the boundary with Worcestershire.

Besides all these events, visitors will come across numerous delightful flower festivals in village churches and many village shows, as they travel about the county.

The tomb of John Abel, King's Carpenter, in Sarnesfield churchyard. The inscriptions are said to have been his work, at the age of ninety.

Herefordshire people

John Abel (1577-1674)

The work of this master architect epitomises the timber-framed buildings which so enrich the Herefordshire landscape. Usually referred to as the 'King's Carpenter', he was granted the style of 'one of his Majesty's carpenters' by Charles I, in recognition of his skill in designing powder and corn mills for the Royalist city of Hereford, under siege by Scottish Parliamentarian forces in 1645.

Much has been attributed to Abel's design without documentary evidence; for example, Hereford Town Hall, demolished in 1862, and Ledbury Market Hall, still standing (see chapter 11). Two outstanding monuments to his talent can still be visited: Grange Court, Leominster (see chapter 11), and the ceilings and sumptuous Jacobean screen at Abbey Dore (see chapter 4). Both date from 1633. Lady Hawkins Grammar School (1625), Kington (see chapter 11), is also by Abel, but is not timber-framed.

Abel is buried in the tree-surrounded little churchyard at Sarnesfield, 2 miles (3 km) south-west of Weobley. His chest tomb was carved, it is said, by his own hand at the age of ninety. The design shows Abel and his two wives, the instruments of his profession and a six-line verse.

Elizabeth Barrett Browning (1806-61).

Principal figure in one of the great romantic stories of English literature, Elizabeth Barrett was brought to Colwall as an infant when her family moved from Durham. A child prodigy, who could read Greek at nine, she revelled in the surrounding countryside, riding her pony across the western slopes of the Malvern Hills above Colwall. Tragedy struck when, at the age of fifteen, a riding accident severely damaged her spine, leaving her a permanent invalid. For five years she was confined to the house at Colwall, appropriately named Hope End, writing poetry which described the garden and hills she could no longer roam. The house was burnt down in 1910.

Reverse followed reverse: her mother died, her father got into financial difficulties and her brother drowned. Her father took a house in Wimpole Street, London, and kept her closely confined, never allowing her out. One caller, however, persisted: Robert Browning, impressed by her poems, continued to visit and eventually, after a secret marriage, they left for Italy. In the Mediterranean climate, improved health and the birth of a son brought happiness to the final fifteen years of Elizabeth's life, and she wrote some of her best poetry.

Ledbury contains two memorials: Mr Barrett's grave and the Barrett Browning Institute (see Ledbury, in chapter 11).

Jane Clifford (c 1134-76)

The 'Fair Rosamund' in Tennyson's 'Dream of Fair Women', Jane Clifford is the subject of another great literary tragedy, but one without a happy ending. Born at Clifford Castle (see chapter 4), her singular beauty attracted the attentions of Henry II, whose queen, Eleanor, was eleven years his senior. To protect his beautiful young mistress from the queen's wrath, so the legend runs, Henry installed Jane in an intricate guarded maze at Woodstock, near Oxford. The precautions were to no avail: while he was away quelling rebellion in France, Eleanor gained access to Jane and forced her to drink poison, thus eliminating the competition in a time-honoured manner.

Sir Edward Elgar (1857-1934)

Born at Lower Broadheath in neighbouring Worcestershire, Elgar is perhaps the best-loved of all English composers. Closely associated with the Three Choirs Festival, which he first visited in 1878 as a violinist, he lived in Hereford from 1904 to 1912. His house there, Plas Gwyn in Hampton Park Road, is now flats. His final appearance in the Three Choirs Festival was at Hereford Cathedral in 1933 as conductor. His great works include the symphonies, the *Enigma Variations* and *The Dream of Gerontius,* but he is best remembered as the composer of 'Land of Hope and Glory'.

An Elgar route is signposted from Hereford, east through Mordiford and Ledbury to join the Worcestershire Elgar route at Little Malvern. Maps and guides are available at the Hereford Tourist Information Office (see chapter 12).

David Garrick (1716-79)

Garrick was born in Hereford, at the Angel Inn, which stood on the corner of Widemarsh and Maylord Streets. The present house on the site bears a plaque. His baptism on 28th February 1716 is recorded in the register of nearby All Saints Church.

Nell Gwynne (1650-87)

Reputedly born in Pipewell Lane, now called Gwynne Street, Hereford (see chapter 11), Nell Gwynne was an actress of some merit, but her main claim to fame is as the mistress of Charles II. Some years after her death one of her grandsons, Bishop Beauclerk, was created Bishop of Hereford and took up residence in the Bishop's Palace, not far from the site of the lowly cottage where Nell may have been born.

Richard Hakluyt (1553-1616)

Richard Hakluyt, of Eyton Old Hall, near Kingsland, can fairly be regarded as the founder of modern geography. A prolific writer on voyages of discovery by explorers of many nationalities, his fame spread across Europe. The Hakluyt family was prominent in Herefordshire over several generations, as sheriffs and members of Parliament. Sir Leonard Hakluyt was with Henry V at Agincourt.

Lady Brilliana Harley (c 1600-43)

A member of the well known Herefordshire family after whom Harley Street in London was named, Lady Brilliana is renowned for her redoubtable defence of Brampton Bryan castle during the Civil War. Her husband, Sir Robert Harley, a prominent Cromwellian, was absent on parliamentary business in London when a strong Royalist force laid siege to the castle. Lady Brilliana rallied the small family force of retainers and tenants and held out for six or seven weeks in 1643, until the besieging forces were called elsewhere. She died a few weeks later. The Royalists captured the castle after a second siege the following year and it was largely destroyed.

Blessed John Kemble (1595-1679)

The martyrdom of this Catholic priest was one of the most shameful episodes of Herefordshire history. The resident priest to the Scudamore family at Pembridge Castle (see chapter 4), Kemble was arrested in 1678 during the Titus Oates scare, taken to Hereford and tried the following year. Despite his harmless nature and advanced age, being over eighty, he was hanged on Widmarsh Common, Hereford. His grave is in Welsh Newton churchyard. The Church of St Francis Xavier, Hereford, has a relic of him.

Stephen Kemble (1758-1822)

Born at Kington, the actor Stephen Kemble was a member of a famous theatrical family. His father, Roger, also an actor, was born in Hereford in 1721 and lived in Leicester Place off Church Street. Stephen's brother John succeeded David Garrick as England's leading actor, while his sister Sarah became the famous Mrs Siddons. Hereford had theatres named after all three of the famous theatrical personalities native to the county, Garrick, Kemble and Nell Gwynne. Two were demolished but the third survives as the New Hereford Theatre.

Reverend Robert Francis Kilvert (1840-79)

An obscure Victorian country parson, Kilvert would have remained unknown but for the diaries he kept from 1870 until 1879 and which gave us detailed accounts of everyday life in a nineteenth-century rural parish and contain delightful personal observations on the countryside and its inhabitants. A native of Wiltshire, Kilvert served as curate from 1865 to 1872 at Clyro, just across the border in Powys, north of Hay-on-Wye, and finally moved into Herefordshire as vicar of Bredwardine (see chapter 11) in 1877. It was to be only a short tenure: having married Elizabeth Rowland of Wootton, Oxfordshire, he returned to Bredwardine in 1879 but he died of peritonitis scarcely a month after the wedding at the age of 38. His grave in Bredwardine churchyard bears the inscription 'He being dead yet speaketh'.

Richard Payne Knight (1750-1824) and Thomas Andrew Knight (1758-1838)

These were two distinguished scholarly brothers whose grandfather had amassed a fortune in ironmaking. Richard was an antiquarian and classical scholar, a trustee of the British Museum. Inheriting the Downton estate from his grandfather, he built an imposing romantic castellated mansion, Downton Castle, in a dramatic setting above the gorge, 4 miles (6 km) west of Ludlow, and laid out the grounds in the Picturesque manner, a challenge and contrast to the softer parkland landscapes of the 'Capability' Brown school.

Thomas was a leading botanist and horticulturalist who poineered a number of techniques for improving the quality of fruit and vegetables, especially apples, cherries and plums. He was elected president of the Royal Horticultural Society in 1820. The imposing chest tombs of these two brothers are in Wormsley churchyard, 8 miles (11 km) north-west of Hereford. A number of unusual cast iron gravestones to other members of the Knight family will be found at Burrington (see chapter 5).

John Kyrle (1637-1724)

A philanthropist and town planner, known popularly as the Man of Ross, John Kyrle's principal monument is the Prospect Garden at Ross-on-Wye, giving a magnificent view across a broad sweep of the river to the Welsh mountains beyond (see Ross-on-Wye, chapter 11). His house stands opposite the stone Town Hall at Ross and there is a portrait of him in the Churchill Gardens Museum, Hereford.

John Masefield (1878-1967)

Born at Ledbury, Masefield was the fifteenth Poet Laureate in a line which began in 1668. He was apprenticed aboard a windjammer but, having sailed around Cape Horn, apparently lost his taste for the seafaring life and remained in the United States for some years leading a precarious existence. His best known and loved poems are on maritime themes, notably 'Sea Fever' and 'Cargoes', but he also wrote adventure novels, children's books and more serious verse: 'Dauber' (1913) concerns the struggle of the visionary against ignorance and materialism. He published an autobiography, *So Long to Learn.* He became Poet Laureate in 1930 and was awarded the Order of Merit in 1933.

Alfred Watkins (1855-1935)

A Hereford man of many parts, Alfred Watkins is chiefly celebrated for his contributions to photography, especially his invention of the exposure meter, and as the author of *The Old Straight Track,* a treatise on so-called 'ley lines' which has aroused widespread interest. As a prominent Hereford businessman he anticipated modern interest in diet by inventing a new type of brown bread. Hereford City Museum (see chapter 7) normally has a display devoted to his photographic inventions.

Thomas Winter (1795-1851)

Thomas Winter, who came from Fownhope, 6 miles (8 km) south-east of Hereford, was a prizefighter better known as Tom Spring. He became champion of England in 1821. He fought in several epic bare-knuckle battles, none harder than his 77 rounds with the Irish champion John Langan at Worcester racecourse in 1824. So great was the throng that the grandstand collapsed. After retirement, Tom Spring was for a time landlord of the Booth Hall tavern, which is still to be found off High Town in Hereford. There is a remote monument to him deep in the Woolhope Hills, south-east of Hereford, reached by a pleasant walk signposted from the Fownhope to Woolhope road.

Ross on Wye market hall is well weathered Old Red Sandstone: the medallion commemorates John Kyrle, the Man of Ross.

A fine range of Georgian farm buildings border the green at Blakemere.

11
Towns and villages

Hereford is much larger than any other settlement in the county, yet it retains much of the air of a country market town, especially on Wednesday when the main livestock market is held. Roads radiate from the city to the market towns, spaced fairly evenly around Herefordshire and each retaining a sense of identity and human scale lost for ever in so many over-large and redeveloped towns in other parts of Britain. There are villages and hamlets, punctuating the main routes, tucked away along secondary roads and hidden deep in little-visited valleys. Infinite variety of form and appearance is the chief glory of the English village and those of Herefordshire are no exception. This chapter lists the best known, together with one or two chosen for particular features: some take a half or even a full day to explore properly, while others can be encompassed in a fifteen-minute stroll, but all are delightful. In travelling around Herefordshire the visitor will encounter many more, smaller villages and hamlets, grouped around churches, bridges and old castle sites, their buildings and way of life little altered since the Tudor period.

BLAKEMERE

Although just a roadside hamlet on B4352, 9 miles (14 km) west of Hereford, Blakemere is visually delightful. The little church of St Leonard is surrounded by several ancient black and white cottages in a good state of preservation. Behind the churchyard the ground drops to a lake, probably the origin of the hamlet name, then rises steeply to Blakemere Hill Wood on the outermost ridge of the Black Mountains. Across the green is an impressive Georgian group of large farmhouse and outbuildings, all in warm red brick, the end of one barn ornamented with an unusually fine diamond-shaped ventilation panel executed in brick.

BOSBURY

Bosbury is a wide one-street village 4 miles (6 km) north of Ledbury on B4220, its large church and several substantial buildings indicating the former prosperity and importance of the place. The manor was owned by the Bishops of Hereford. The massive church tower is detached and of fortress-like proportions; the main church building is equally impressive with splendid roof beams and a wealth of good monuments and rich furnishings. Adjacent to the churchyard is Old Court House, formerly the country house of the Bishops of Hereford. Nearby are the former Elizabethan free grammar school (1540) and the village inn, once the home of the Harford family, lords of the manor.

BROMYARD
Early closing Tuesday; market day Thursday.

The car park is at the western end of the High Street: to reach the Tourist Information Centre turn left along to Rowberry Street (chapter 12), then return to High Street for a leisurely stroll through a typical local market town, happily bypassed by the A44. The Falcon Hotel, midway along on the right, is the street's most pleasing building, timber-framed with closely set studding, and the street then curves round to enter the small Market Place, dominated by the nineteenth-century, bay-windowed facade of the Hop Pole Hotel. Opposite, on the south side of the square, a finely decorated, tall timber-framed building formerly served as the town library and is now an interesting studio. Enter Church Street from the north-west corner of the square and walk along to St Peter's Church, mainly fourteenth-century but with surviving Norman work and an interesting exterior castellated stair turret to the tower. There are an unusual number of tomb recesses, all fourteenth-century, both inside and out. Bromyard's best house is Tower Hill House (1630) at the junction of Pump Street and the bypass, a large, ornately decorated timber-framed building, where Charles I stayed in 1644.

CRADLEY
Cradley is a pretty black and white street village on the extreme eastern boundary of Herefordshire, where wooded slopes begin a long ascent to the Malvern ridge. St James's Church is mainly nineteenth-century but there are surviving remnants of earlier periods, particularly an Anglo-Saxon frieze on the north exterior wall of the Norman west tower. Far more pleasing to the eye than the church are the timber-framed lychgate and the fine fifteenth-century parish hall in a corner of the churchyard. Formerly a boys' grammar school, it is a long square-framed building with diagonal braces and a jettied upper floor. Other pleasant timber cottages lie along the road nearby.

DILWYN
The archetypal village scene can be found here: pub, shop and cottages grouped round a small green, with a spreading chestnut tree for good measure. In St Mary's Church nearby the

Bromyard market place has this ornate and well restored sixteenth-century town house, now a countryside art gallery.

medieval roodscreen contains a lovely panel of fourteenth-century glass depicting two angels swinging a censer. A footpath, starting from the gate, leads up a steep field to give good views across the village and surrounding countryside. Weary visitors can enjoy the same view where the footpath reaches the bypass.

DORSTONE

Located at the head of the Golden Valley in the Black Mountains 6 miles (9 km) east of Hay-on-Wye, the village is surprisingly grouped around its village green, an unusual arrangement for this upland area. Church, school, shops, cottages and inn face each other across the triangular market place, which contains a pleasant fountain and a market cross with sundial. Behind the school is a castle mound and a mile to the north on Dorstone Hill is Herefordshore's oldest man-made structure, Arthur's Stone (see chapter 3). Another mile south-east of the village are the remains of Snodhill Castle (see chapter 4). St Faith's Church was heavily restored in 1889 but contains, among other relics, a rare coffin chalice of the thirteenth century. St Faith's was reputedly founded by John de Brito as a penance for his part in the murder of Thomas Becket in 1171.

EARDISLAND

This is Herefordshire's film-set village, the subject of innumerable calendar and chocolate-box illustrations, located on the A44, 5 miles (8 km) west of Leominster. The river Arrow flows placidly between well tended gardens and timber-framed houses, an attraction for both visitors and artists, all welcomed by the large, raucous and apparently ever hungry duck population. East of the bridge, facing the river, is Staick House, its central portion a fourteenth-century yeoman's hall, unusual in that its roof survives with an almost complete set of sandstone tiles. Beside the bridge is the timber-framed former grammar school: one of the supporting timbers still has manacles affixed, from the days when it served as the village whipping post.

West of the bridge is a second smaller bridge over the millstream. Here is a four-gabled dovecote, seventeenth-century brick-built, its three-storeyed double wall accommodating some eight hundred nesting alcoves. The dovecote stands in a corner of the walled garden of the Manor House, a large timber-framed house of the seventeenth century with a massive stone chimney breast and the surprising addition of a brick-built Queen Anne wing facing the road.

Opposite, beside the Cross Inn, take the lane to St Mary's Church with its fine timber-raftered thirteenth-century nave. From the north-east corner of the churchyard is a view of the moated mound on which a small wooden castle would have stood, guarding the crossing of the Arrow in this troubled border region. A mile south of the village is Burton Court (see chapter 6).

EASTNOR

This is a wholly delightful estate village grouped round the entrance to Eastnor Castle

At Eardisland the large duck population are always ready to abandon the river Arrow to demand food from visitors and residents alike.

grounds (see chapter 6), 2 miles (3 km) east of Ledbury, all dating from the mid nineteenth century. The church of St John is largely the work of Sir Giles Gilbert Scott (1852) but the tower is fourteenth-century and there are Norman remnants. The interior is well furnished with memorials and the churchyard contains a seat with reliefs designed by Lady Somerset of Eastnor Castle. The village well on the green with its terracotta reliefs in the Italian Renaissance style is also her design. A rectory, post office, former school and estate cottages, all of the mid nineteenth century, complete this textbook example of Victorian paternalism in village design.

HAY-ON-WYE
Early closing Tuesday; market day Thursday,
Follow the signs to the main car park then set off to explore this delightful border town, just inside Wales but part of the itinerary of everyone visiting Herefordshire and the Black Mountains. A maze of narrow streets and alleys crowds the steep slope between the ruined castle and the river Wye, each street given a character of its own by the cosmopolitan collection of craft and book shops drawn to set up business in the town. It is the extraordinary concentration of second-hand bookshops which draws people time and again to Hay: there are at least a dozen, catering for all tastes and budgets, from paperbacks by the yard to rare antiquarian volumes, first editions and fine prints. The town's former cinema, converted and extended, is claimed to be the world's largest second-hand bookshop, with over a quarter of a million volumes. As well as books, there are shops selling antiques and bygones, potteries and interesting eating places. A town to savour at a leisurely pace, Hay is also the gateway to the Black Mountains.

HEREFORD
No early closing day for most shops; main livestock market on Wednesday.
The walk described here encompasses the main items of interest in the historic city centre. Visitors are strongly recommended to use the Wye Street car park immediately south of Wye Bridge (149: 508396). Should this be full, a second car park lies about 150 yards (140 metres) south: see map on page 47.

Wye Bridge (late fifteenth century) provides an excellent view of the cathedral. Immediately downstream was the ford which gave the city its name. Hereford means 'army ford', the place where a *herepath,* or army road, crossed a river. The banks on either side here were lined with warehouses and boatyards in the days of the Wye navigation. Walk north from the bridge and in about 30 yards (27 metres)

Hay-on-Wye clock tower is a focal point in the maze of narrow streets.

turn right into the narrow **Gwynne Street.** A plaque in the high wall on the right marks the approximate site of the reputed birthplace of Nell Gwynne (see chapter 10); a tall warehouse on the left is a reminder of the large amount of traffic formerly carried on the Wye. Gwynne Street opens out to provide a first class view of **Hereford Cathedral,** although the west front (by John Oldrid Scott, 1902-8) is not its best aspect, being a rather uninspired version of early twentieth-century Decorated revivalism. Immediately right at the end of Gwynne Street is the arched gateway to the **Bishop's Palace.**

Before exploring the Cathedral, visitors may like to absorb something of the atmosphere of central Hereford by following **Broad Street,** directly ahead, with All Saints' Church at the far end. Notable buildings in Broad Street include the **City Museum and Art Gallery** (1874) on the left, facing the Cathedral, **St Francis Xavier Roman Catholic Church** (1839) with two impressive columns on the right, followed by a pleasant canopy of cast iron reaching across the pavement, now part of the **National Westminster Bank Building** (1863). The **Green Dragon Hotel** (1857) has a long, striking facade and finally, on the right,

All Saints Church and Broad Street, Hereford.

Barclays Bank (1790) was originally a town house for the Duke of Norfolk.

All Saints' Church (see chapter 5), mainly of the thirteenth and fourteenth centuries, is worth exploring and notable chiefly for its collection of chained books, the second largest anywhere. It is remarkable that the world's largest collection is housed at the other end of Broad Street, in the Cathedral. Return along Broad Street to the **Cathedral** and enter by the north porch (see Chapter 5). As with any large ecclesiastical building a guidebook is necessary to get the best from a visit. The Cathedral contains the superb Chained Library and the Treasury in the crypt (see chapter 7 for both). Another unique possession not to be missed is Mappa Mundi (late thirteenth-century), a fanciful world map executed on vellum. Leave the Cathedral by the north porch and cross the close to **Church Street,** a delightful medieval alley with interesting shops, including those in **Capuchin Yard,** halfway along on the left.

High Town is the large pedestrianised area at the end of Church Street. Immediately opposite is the **Butter Market** (1861), always a centre of bustling activity and a useful shelter in rainy weather. **The Old House** (1621) is a museum (see chapter 7) and stands on its own, diagonally across High Town to the left as you leave the Butter Market. It is the only surviv-

ing building of Butchers Row, the others being swept away in 1837. Beyond the Old House is **St Peter's Square** with the city's **war memorial** as its centrepiece. **St Peter's Church** (see chapter 6) is basically early fourteenth-century, heavily restored. The main interest in this area lies in the two centres of local government, the **Shire Hall** by Smirke (1819) and the **Town Hall** by Cheers (1904). Both are well worth looking at, inside and out: they provide a fascinating comparison between the concepts of municipal architecture at the beginning and close of the nineteenth century (see chapter 7). Custodians in each building can be contacted to show the main points of interest. **Hereford Tourist Information Centre** adjoins the Town Hall (see chapter 12).

Go through the Town Hall into **East Street,** cross diagonally to the right and follow a narrow, walled footpath to the north-east corner of **Cathedral Close.** From here you may either return across the Close to Gwynne Street and your starting point or continue the walk. To continue, turn left along the front of the houses facing the Close and left again out of the large iron gates into **Castle Street,** a wide elegant thoroughfare with a predominantly Georgian air. Turn right into **Quay Street,** beside the **Cathedral School.** Notice on the left in about 75 yards (70 metres) the

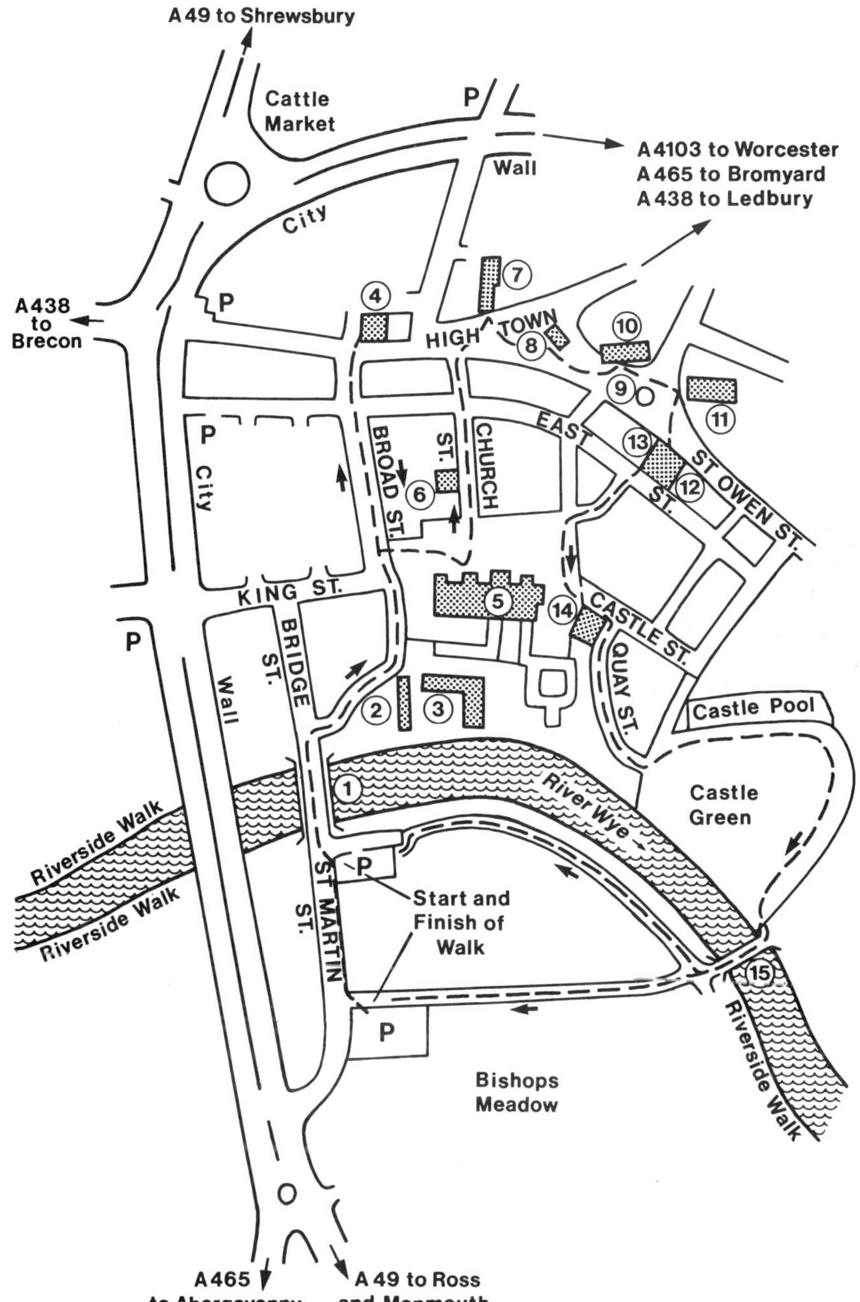

HEREFORD CITY CENTRE. *1 Wye Bridge. 2 Gwynne Street. 3 Bishop's Palace. 4 All Saints Church. 5 Cathedral. 6 Capuchin Yard. 7 Butter Market. 8 Old House. 9 St Peter's Square. 10 St Peter's Church. 11 Shire Hall. 12 Town Hall. 13 Tourist Information Centre. 14 Cathedral School. 15 Suspension bridge (pedestrian).*

admirably restored **School Tuck Shop,** winner of a conservation award.

Next comes **Castle Green,** the site of Hereford Castle (see chapter 4), which originated before the Norman conquest but was razed in Welsh raids in 1055. William Fitzosborn rebuilt it in motte and bailey style but nothing now remains except the substantial earth embankment which surrounded the bailey. This is a pleasant open space with a bowling green and a 60 foot (18 metres) high column erected in 1809 to commemorate Lord Nelson's naval victories. Nelson received the freedom of Hereford in 1802 and it had been intended to commission a statue to surmount the column. Funds ran out, however, and a less expensive urn was substituted.

From the elevated walk along the south side of Castle Green there are good views across the Wye. Take the fine cast iron pedestrian suspension footbridge, **Victoria Bridge** (1898), to **Bishop's Meadow.** Turn sharp right along the river bank for the car park near Wye Bridge or half-right for the further car park.

The **livestock market** is well worth visiting, especially on Wednesday mornings. This is the hub of livestock dealing for the county which has exported its cattle all over the world. There are several car parks around the market. Visit the main sale ring with its tiered seating to hear the auctioneer rattling out his patter through the microphone.

There are a number of other museums which should not be missed (see chapter 7).

Guided walks around the historic centre of Hereford are provided by members of the Hereford Guild of Guides: information from the Tourist Information Centre next to the Town Hall (chapter 12).

HOARWITHY

A pleasant riverside village on the steep-sided banks of the Wye 8 miles (12 km) south-east of Hereford, Hoarwithy has an extraordinary Italianate church (see chapter 5) and a charming village inn. The bridge with its Gothic toll house is a good point from which to view the river and walk its banks.

KILPECK

Students of the English village will find this one of the most rewarding sites in the land: all the elements of the Norman village are here, virtually uncluttered by subsequent additions. Located just south of A465, 8 miles (12 km) south-west of Hereford, Kilpeck has one of England's finest small Norman churches (see chapter 5), a motte and bailey castle site (see chapter 4), nearby cottages and farm and the site of a priory. There are good all-round views from the castle mound.

KING'S PYON

In rich farming country 8 miles (12 km) north-west of Hereford, just west of A4110, with the large church of St Mary dominating the view from a high mound, this is another quiet little village. Along the village street is an impressive timber-framed dovecote with a glazed lantern. A mile south-east is neighbouring Canon Pyon church, its tower leaning at a worrying angle: at the churchyard entrance is a rare survival, a stone cattle pound for confining stray cattle. The name Pyon is apparently derived from the Saxon *Peon,* a disease-infested swamp.

KINGTON

Early closing Wednesday; market days Tuesday and Thursday.

Now bypassed by A44, visitors can enjoy a stroll along the main street unpolluted by exhaust fumes. The town is located on a spur between the river Arrow and its tributary Gilwern Brook, with the large St Mary's Church occupying the highest point of the ridge. Near the church are Lady Hawkins Grammar School, designed by John Abel (see chapter 10) but not timber-framed, and Hergest Croft Gardens (see chapter 6). Lady Hawkins was the wife of Sir John Hawkins, commander of the English fleet against the Spanish Armada and infamous for having laid the foundations of the slave trade. At the bottom of the hill, where High Street starts, is the Victorian Market Hall (1885), which replaced one built by John Abel in 1654. The tower above the market was erected in 1897 to mark Victoria's Diamond Jubilee. All around is good upland walking country (see chapter 2) on Hergest Ridge and Bradnor Hill.

LEDBURY

Early closing Wednesday; livestock market Wednesday.

A good town-centre car park is opposite the timbered Market Hall, behind St Katherine's almshouses. Delightfully situated on the lower slopes of wooded hills, Ledbury is the textbook market town, worthy of savouring at a leisurely pace for its superb timber-framed architecture and its literary associations. Leave the car park between the fourteenth-century St Katherine's Hospital and the nineteenth-century almshouses to emerge into the High Street, here very wide where it served as a market place. Immediately opposite is the impressive Market House, supported on sixteen tall pillars of Spanish chestnut. Built between about 1620 and 1660, it has been attributed to John Abel (see chapter 10) but without documentary proof. To the left is the clock tower of the Barrett Browning Memorial Institute. See chapter 10 for the town's association with Elizabeth Barrett

ABOVE: *Market House, Ledbury.*

RIGHT: *Feathers Hotel, Ledbury.*

Browning.

Behind the Market House is the start of Church Street, one of England's best preserved medieval alleys, with cobbled roadway and jettied timber-framed buildings along both sides. First come the fifteenth-century former council offices, then the Ledbury Heritage Centre (see chapter 7), housed in the old grammar school (about 1500), and Butcher Row House, containing a folk museum (see chapter 7). At the top of the street is impressive Church House, about 1600. Here enter the peaceful precincts of St Michael's Church (see chapter 5).

Returning to the Market House, turn left to follow the gradually narrowing High Street up to the town's main crossroads, passing the Feathers Hotel, about 1560-70. At the crossroads, the massive Ledbury Park is one of Herefordshire's finest timber-framed houses. On the opposite corner another good example is supported on timber posts across the pavement, in constant danger from heavy goods vehicles in the narrowly confined street. Along

49

Leintwardine.

this street is the Talbot Hotel, another late sixteenth-century, timber-framed building.

Having explored Ledbury, lovers of railway architecture may wish to visit the station to view the end of the tunnel where the Hereford-Worcester line plunges deep into the hillside. The superb viaduct across the Leadon valley can be seen from the A438 just outside the town at 149: 702387.

LEINTWARDINE

A large village with a long history, Leintwardine lies on the A4113, 13 miles (18 km) north-west of Leominster. The Romans had their settlement of *Bravonium* here (see chapter 3), where Watling Street West, the north-south borderland military road, crossed the river Teme, just downstream from its confluence with the river Clun. There is evidence too, that it was a planned Norman settlement, with two parallel main north-south streets and several connecting secondary streets and alleys. By the present bridge across the Teme there is a pleasant green. Park here and walk uphill to the large church of St Mary Magdalene. It is said that the choir stalls came from the now almost vanished Wigmore Abbey, 3 miles (5 km) south of the village and the reputed resting place of several members of the great Mortimer family. From the church, wander through the various streets back down to the river. There are numerous interesting houses and pleasant small shops.

LEOMINSTER
Early closing Thursday; market day Friday.

This is Herefordshire's second town, 13 miles (21 km) north of Hereford on the A49 and the focal point for commerce in north Herefordshire. The car park in Etnam Street (the A44 leading to Worcester) provides a convenient point from which to explore the historic centre of Leominster. Leave by the pedestrian access to The Grange, a pleasant tree-lined playing field area with a raised walk on its southern perimeter, part of the former town defences: as a border town, Leominster had a long history of turbulence from Welsh raids. Turn right and follow this walk to Grange Court, the fine timbered building in a garden on the northern side of The Grange.

John Abel (see chapter 10) built Grange Court in 1633 as the Market House and it stood in the town centre at the northern end of High Street. When a new town hall was built in 1855 the Market House was sold to a member of the Arkwright family, dismantled and re-erected on its present site as a private residence. The lower storey was originally open-sided between the pillars. With its abundance of rich carvings, Grange Court is one of the showpieces of timber-frame architecture in Herefordshire.

On the far side of The Grange is the Priory Church (see chapter 5), at one time the core of an extensive complex of monastic buildings (see chapter 4). From the churchyard the main gate leads into Church Street with some fine Georgian buildings. Halfway along on the right is Forbury Chapel, now used commercially but originally the thirteenth-century chapel of St Thomas Becket. At the end of Church Street, turn left into the pedestrianised medieval Draper's Lane, with interesting narrow passageways through to High Street.

Emerge into Corn Square, scene of a lively market each Friday, and cross diagonally to Old School Lane with its overhanging medieval timber-framed buildings housing interesting little shops and Leominster Tourist Information Centre. The Folk Museum (see chapter 7) is opposite the end of Old School Lane, in Etnam Street.

LINGEN

Lingen is a delightful little village hidden deep in the hills 12 miles (17 km) north-west of Leominster, where England merges into Wales. At the north end of the street is St Michael's Church, largely restored in the nineteenth century but with pleasant rough-hewn oak pews remaining from the earlier church. Nearby is the mound of a motte and bailey castle and a mile south are the scant remains of Limebrook Priory (see chapter 4). Lingen was the site of a seventeenth-century pottery industry.

MANSELL LACY

This enjoyable estate village off the A480, 5 miles (7 km) north-west of Hereford, is grouped by the gateway to Foxley Estate, formerly the home of Sir Uvedale Price (1747-1829), a prime exponent of the English Picturesque school of landscaping. The house is now gone but much of the surrounding woodland is a testament to his concepts. There are family memorials in Yazor church, now closed, a mile west along the main road, and just beyond the church, up the minor road, is an archway which took the estate carriage drive over the deep cutting. South of the main road (at 404465) are the ruins of Yazor old church, reached through a farmyard.

MORDIFORD

Park in the lay-by across the bridge from the church, on the B4224, 4 miles (6 km) east of Hereford. Facing the river is the rectory, well proportioned early Georgian. The bridge is Herefordshire's oldest, one arch of the fourteenth century with a massive cutwater. It is approached by a causeway: the Lugg rises dramatically in times of flood. Note on the bridge the iron ties binding the parapet stones together and the stone plaque 'HCC1': this was the first on the county's register of bridges. The village street curves round with a delightful terrace of old cottages, now well below modern road level. The church has a Norman doorway and good views across the Lugg valley.

From the lay-by there is a riverside walk downstream to the confluence of the Lugg and the Wye. Nearby is Sufton Court (see chapter 6).

PEMBRIDGE

Formerly a market town on A44, 7 miles (11

This quaint house at Mansell Lacy incorporates a dovecote or pigeon loft in its gabled end.

Riverside meadows at Ross-on-Wye: the town occupies the higher ground beyond.

km) west of Leominster, Pembridge has a wealth of timber-framed buildings in most styles. Park in the market place with its open sixteenth-century Market House, which formerly had an upper storey. Nearby is the seventeenth-century New Inn, a staging post on the Worcester to Aberystwyth road. A flight of steps leads up from the market place to the spacious churchyard, cleared of all its old gravestones to provide a delightful grassy setting for the church and its unique detached bell-tower (see chapter 5).

Leave the churchyard on its lower side, down another flight of cobbled steps beside the shop, a large early sixteenth-century house with an intricately carved pair of barge-boards on the gable end facing down the street. Explore both east and west along the main street: there are fine timbered houses, rows of cottages and, at the eastern end of the village, Trafford's Almhouses (1686) with quaint inscriptions.

From the centre of the village, opposite the shop, Bridge Street runs down to the river Arrow. Here you can park and picnic upstream or downstream of the bridge, a delightfully cool and peaceful spot on a hot summer afternoon.

PENCOMBE

Well away from any main road, this pleasant little village is tucked in the rolling hills 4 miles (6 km) south-west of Bromyard. St John's church is nineteenth-century but contains some older furnishings and an interesting tablet to Richard Jordan, a local man who perished in 1832 on an expedition to survey the river Niger with the explorer Richard Lander of Truro, who also died, shot by a native. The village groups attractively round the green, with a large memorial cross as its centrepiece.

ROSS-ON-WYE

Early closing Wednesday; market days Thursday and Saturday; livestock market Friday.

The main town of south Herefordshire, Ross-on-Wye is a base for exploring the glories of the lower Wye Valley and the Forest of Dean, as well as Herefordshire. The historic town centre, with narrow steep streets, clusters about the church (see chapter 5) on a steep red sandstone cliff overlooking a huge loop of the Wye. The main visitor car park is down at river level on the causeway approaching the town from Wilton Bridge (1597). From here it is a steep climb up to the church but rewarding in providing the opportunity to admire the landscaping of the grounds above the cliff. The summit has The Prospect, part of public gardens laid out by John Kyrle (see chapter 10) in 1693, entered by a dignified pillared gate of 1700. The view from the gardens is splendid, across the Wye Valley to the hills far into Wales on a clear day.

Nearby is the crowded triangular Market

Place with the seventeenth-century Market Hall of much weathered local red sandstone and John Kyrle's house on the opposite side of the narrow street. Down on the river bank, across the road from the car park, are extensive public gardens and meadow land, an ideal picnic area.

SYMONDS YAT

Symonds Yat East is approached by a minor road off B4229, 5 miles (8 km) south-west of Ross-on-Wye. There is also Symonds Yat West on the opposite bank of the Wye. Neither is a true village: they are rather scatterings of houses where the Wye Valley becomes a dramatic gorge. plunging into the carboniferous rocks of the Forest of Dean. The area is extremely congested in summer, but there are unlimited forest and riverside walks, besides various tourist attractions (see chapter 7) and visitor facilities in the vicinity.

WEOBLEY

Just off A4112, 8 miles (12 km) south-west of Leominster, Weobley has, like neighbouring Pembridge 5 miles (8 km) to the north, the feel of a small town and has declined greatly in importance since the days when it sent two members to Parliament. Park on the broad main street and walk, first to the northern end where the soaring spire of the church of Saints Peter and Paul (see chapter 5) rises behind the Red Lion Hotel and the immaculate bowling green. Return up Broad Street; the triangular garden at the top was formerly the site of several buildings, including a large mansion house. Immediately ahead a footpath leads through a pleasant avenue to the castle site (see chapter 4), where only the impressive earthworks remain. Beyond, there are walks across the open countryside of the Garnstone Estate.

Lovers of timber-framed building will find the short detour to view The Ley rewarding. Take B4230 leading south from Weobley and turn right along the minor road at the top of the hill. It is not signposted, and the road is a cul-de-sac. The Ley dates from 1589 and is a tall, impressively gabled country house with the beams left in their original unpainted state.

WHITNEY ON WYE

Here a fine wooden toll bridge carries the B4530 over the river Wye.

WOOLHOPE

Another remote village with a timeless air, well away from any main road yet only 6 miles

Weobley.

Massive wooden piers have supported Whitney on Wye toll bridge since the 1820s. Previous structures had collapsed in times of flood.

(9 km) south-east of Hereford, Woolhope is tucked into a valley in the centre of the Woolhope Dome, a notable geological formation of concentric ridges and valleys where the older Silurian limestones and shales have been forced up through the much later Old Red Sandstone comprising most of lowland Herefordshire. Woolhope has all the classic village elements: fine old church, pub, and combined shop and post office. The church has a good collection of coffin lids of the thirteenth and fourteenth centuries. Nearby Haugh Wood and Broadmoor Common (see chapter 2) provide excellent walking.

YARPOLE

Yarpole is a pretty village 5 miles (8 km) north-west of Leominster, with a stream running through its centre, and a number of very attractive timbered buildings including a medieval gatehouse known as the Bakehouse on the stream bank. The church was partly rebuilt in the nineteenth century but substantial fragments from the early fourteenth century remain. The detached bell-tower, supported by a framework of massive oak posts and beams, is not quite as impressive as the example at Pembridge (see above and chapter 5) but is more complete.

12
Tourist information centres

Bromyard: Council Offices, 1 Rowberry Street, Bromyard, Herefordshire. Telephone: Bromyard (0885) 82341. Monday to Friday, all year.

Hay-on-Wye: The Car Park, Hay-on-Wye, Powys. Telephone: Hay-on-Wye (0497) 820144. Every day, Easter to end of September.

Hereford: Town Hall Annexe, St Owen Street, Hereford HR1 2PJ. Telephone: Hereford (0432) 268430. Monday to Saturday in summer; Monday to Friday in winter.

Kington: Council Offices, 2 Mill Street, Kington, Herefordshire: Telephone: Kington (0544) 230202. Daily in summer; Mondays, Tuesdays and Fridays in winter.

Ledbury: Council Offices, St Katherine's, Ledbury, Herefordshire. Telephone: Ledbury (0531) 2461. Monday to Friday, all year.

Leominster: 6 School Lane, Leominster, Herefordshire. Telephone: Leominster (0568) 2291. Monday to Saturday in summer; Monday to Friday in winter.

Ross-on-Wye: Wyedean Tourist Board, 20 Broad Street, Ross-on-Wye, Herefordshire. Telephone: Ross-on-Wye (0989) 62768. Daily in summer; Monday to Friday in winter.

HEREFORDSHIRE and the Black Mountains
Leintwardine
R. Teme
Mortimer Forest
Burrington
Mary Knoll Valley
Wigmore Castle
Croft Ambrey
Bircher Common
Lingen
Limebrook Priory
Fishpool Valley
Croft Castle
Stapleton Castle
Aymestrey
Yarpole
Berrington Hall
Mortimer's Cross
Shobdon
R. Lugg
Horseway Herbs
Rowe Ditch
Eardisland
LEOMINSTER
Lower Brockhampton
Stanner Rocks
Offa's Dyke
Pembridge
Bromyard Downs
Bringsty Common
R. Arrow
Burton Court
BROMYARD
Hergest Croft
KINGTON
Dilwyn
Hergest Ridge
Pencombe
Westhope Hill
Broadfield Court Vineyards
Weobley
MC
Cwmmau Farmhouse
King's Pyon
Dinmore Manor
Stoke Lacy
Storridge
Cradley
Whitney on Wye
Mansell Lacy
Brinsop
R. Lugg
Clifford Castle
Brobury Garden
Bosbury
Bredwardine
Arthur's Stone
R. Wye
Moccas Court
The Weir
HAY-ON-WYE
Dorstone
Blakemere
HEREFORD
Herefordshire Beacon
Snodhill Castle
Tyberton
Sufton Court
LEDBURY
Midsummer Hill
Peterchurch
Mordiford
Eastnor
Hay Bluff
Vowchurch
Dinedor
Woolhope
Haugh Wood
MALVERN HILLS
BLACK
MOUNTAINS
Bacton
Brockhampton
Hellens
Much Marcle
Olchon Valley
Capler Camp
Abbey Dore
Kilpeck
Hoarwithy
R. Wye
Longtown Castle
ROSS-ON-WYE
Llanthony Abbey
Kentchurch Court
Garway
Pembridge Castle
Goodrich Castle
King Arthur's Cave
Symonds Yat

* Countryside sites (Ch. 2)
⊓ Places of archaeological interest (Ch. 3)
C Castles (Ch. 4)
A Monastic ruins (Ch. 4)
+ Churches (Ch. 5)
▲ Historic houses and Gardens (Ch. 6)
M Museums and other places of interest (Ch. 7)
X Cider makers (Ch. 8)
■ Towns and villages (Ch. 11)

Index

Page numbers in italic refer to illustrations.

Abbey Dore 15-16, 39
Court Garden 27-8
Abel, John 15, *38*, 39, *50*
Adam, Robert 27
Archenfield 4
Arthur's Stone 11, *11*, 44
Aymestrey Gorge 6
Aymestrey church 17
Bacton church 17
Barrett Browning, Elizabeth 19, 39
Barrett Browning Memorial Institute 39, 48
Battlefield site, Mortimer's Cross 32
Bennington Hall 23, *23*
Bircher Common 6
Blackfriars Monastery 16
Black Hill 8
Black Mountains *4*, 5, 7, 8, 16, 42, 44, 45
Blakemere 42, *42*
Bodenham 28
Bosbury 42-3
Vineyards and Gardens 28
Bradnor Hill 6, 8, 28, 48
Brampton Bryan 40
Bredwardine 11, 28, 40
church 17
Bridge Sollars 38
Brilley 25
Bringsty 26-7
Common 6, 27
Brinsop church 17-18
Broadfield Court Vineyards 28
Broadmoor Common 7
Brobury Garden and Gallery 28
Brockhampton church 18
Brockhampton Woodland Walk 6
Bromyard 9, 43, *43*, 54
Downs 6, 27
Folk Festival 38
Gala 38
Bronsil Castle 26
Brown, 'Capability' 23, 27
Bulmer, Percy 34
Bulmer Railway Centre 29, *30*
Burrington church 18, 40
Burton Court 23-4, 44
Bush Bank 10
Butcher Row House 31-2, 49
Capler Camp 11-12
Churchill Gardens Museum and Hatton Gallery 29, 40
Cider 5, 30-1, 34-6
Clifford Castle 4, 13
Clifford, Jane 13, 39
Colwall 39
Cradley 43
Craswall Priory 16
Croft Ambrey 6, 7, 12, 25
Croft Castle 24-5, *24*
Cwmmau Farmhouse 25
Dilwyn 43-4
Dinedor Camp 12
Dinedor Hill 6-7, 12
Dinmore Hill 8-9, 10, 25
Dinmore Manor 25
Dinmore Preceptory 16
Dorstone 11, 44
Downton 40
Dunkerton's Cider Company 35-6

Eardisland *cover*, 23, 44, *44*
Eastnor 44-5
Castle 25-6, *25*, 38
Elgar, Sir Edward 37, 39
Elgar route 39
Ewyas, Vale of *3*, 5, 8, 16
Fishpool Valley 6, 7, 24
Flanesford Priory 16
Fownhope 11, 41
Garrick, David 39
Garway church 18
Garway Hill 26
Golden Valley 14, 17, 20, 28, 44
Goodrich 10
Castle 13, *13*
Great Doward 33
Grange Court 39, 50
Gwynne, Nell 39-40
Hakluyt, Richard 40
Hampton Bishop 10
Hanter Hill 6
Harley, Lady Brilliana 40
Haugh Wood 7
Hay Bluff 7
Hay-on-Wye 10, 37, 45, *45*, 54
Hellens 20, 26
Hereford 3, 10, 18, 39, 40, 41, 42, 45-8, *46*, 54
and West of England Rose Show 37
Antiques Fayre 38
Castle site 14, *14*
Cathedral *17*, 18
Cathedral Chained Library 29
Cathedral Treasury 29
Cattle *1*, 4-5, *37*, 48
City Museum and Art Gallery 12, *29*, 30, 41, 45
defences 12
May Fair 37
Regatta 37
Shire Hall 31, 46
Town Hall 31, 46
Herefordshire and Border Counties Aero Model Rally 38
Herefordshire Beacon 7, 12
Herefordshire Country Fair 38
Herefordshire Music Festival 37
Herefordshire Regimental Museum 30
Herefordshire Rural Heritage Museum 33
Herefordshire school of sculpture 19
Herefordshire Waterworks Museum 30
Hergest Croft Gardens 8, 28, 48
Hergest Ridge 6, 7, 8, 28, 48
Hillforts 3, 6, 7, 8, 11, 12
Hoarwithy 18-19, 48
Hole-in-the-Wall 10
Holland, Henry 23
Hollybush Hill 8
Hope under Dinmore 10
Hops 5
Horseway Herb Garden 28
How Caple 10
Jubilee Maze 33
Kemble, Blessed John 14, 40
Kemble, Stephen 40
Kenchester 10, 11
Kentchurch Court 26
Kerne Bridge 10, 16

Kilpeck 19, *19*, 48
Castle 14
Kilvert, Reverend Francis 17, 28, 40
King Arthur's Cave 12
Kingsland 40
King's Pyon 48
Kington 7, 8, 12, 28, 40, 48, 54
Festival and Eisteddfod 37
Show and Horse Show 38
Knighton 12
Knight, Richard Payne and Thomas Andrew 18, 40
Knights Cider 36
Kyrle, John 20, 40, *41*, 52
Ladies' Raft Race 38
Lady Hawkins Grammar School 39, 48
Ledbury 5, 31-2, 40, 48-50, *49*, 54
church 19
Heritage Centre 32, 49
Hop Fair 38
Market Hall 48
Park 49
Leintwardine 11, 50, *50*
Leominster 4, 23, 39, 50-1, 54
church 19-20
Folk Museum 32, 51
Priory 16
Show and Ledbury Carnival 38
Lethaby, W. R. 18
Ley, The 53
Limebrook Priory 16, 51
Lingen 16, 51
Llanthony Abbey 16, *16*
Longtown Castle 14
Lower Brockhampton 26-7, *27*
Madley Festival 38
Malvern Hills 5, 7-8, 12, 43
Mansell Lacy 51, *51*
Marcher Lords 4
Marches Forest 8
Mary Knoll Valley 8
Masefield, John 40-1
Merlin's Cave 12
Midsummer Hill 7, 8, 12
Moccas Court 27
Monnow Valley 18
Monument Inn 32
Mordiford 10, 27, 51
Mortimer's Cross 4, 24, 32, *32*
Much Marcle 20, *20*, 26, *26*, 36
Museum of Cider 30-1, 35
Museum of the Weobley Historical Society 33
Offa's Dyke 12
Association 8
Path 8
Olchon Valley 8
Old House, Hereford 31
Old Sufton 27
Pembridge 38, 51-2
Castle 14, *15*, 40
church 20, *21*
Pencombe 52
Peterchurch 20-1
Pritchard, Thomas Farnolls 24
Pugin, W. 26
Queen's Wood 8-9
Repton, Humphry 27
River Wye Raft Race 37
'Roaring Meg' mortar 13, 29

Ross-on-Wye 10, 15, 38, 40, *41*, 52-3, *52*, 54
church 21
Rowe Ditch 12
Rushock Hill *8*
St John and Coningsby Medieval Museum 16, 31
Sarnesfield *38*, 39
School Wood 17
Seddon, J. P. 19
Seven Sisters Rocks 12
Shobdon 21, *22*
Smirke, Sir Robert 25
Snodhill Castle 14, 44
Spring, Tom 41
Staick House 44
Stanner Rocks 6, 9, 28
Stapleton Castle 15
Staunton-on-Arrow 28
Stoke Lacy 36
Stoke Lacy Herb Garden 28
Storridge 36
Sufton Court 27, 51
Symonds Cider and English Wine Company 36
Symonds Yat *9*, 53
Bird Park 33
chain ferry *33*
East 10
Rock 9
West 32-3
Swainshill 28
Teme Valley Leisure Drive 9
Three Choirs Festival 37
Three Counties Show 38
Tyberton church 21-2
Vale of Arrow Trotting Races 37
Vowchurch 22, *22*
Watkins, Alfred 41
Weir, The, Swainshill 28
Welsh Newton 14, 40
Weobley 53, *53*
Castle site 15
church 22
museum 33
Westhope Hill 9-10
West Malvern 8
Weston, H. and Sons Ltd 36
Weston under Penyard 11
Whitchurch 12, 33
Whitney on Wye 25, 53, *54*
Wigmore Abbey 50
Wigmore anticline 8
Wigmore Castle 4, 15
Williams-Ellis, Sir Clough 24
Wilton Castle 15
Winter, Thomas 41
Wood, John 21
Woolhope 53-4
Club 11
Dome 7, 54
Hills 27, 41
Wordsworth, William 17
World of Butterflies 33
Wormsley 40
Wyatt, James 27
Wyche Cutting 8
Wye coracles 16
Wye Valley Visitor Centre 33
Wye Valley Walk 10
Wynds Point 8
Yarpole 24, 54
Yazor 51